Love bites

The Unofficial Saga of Twilight

Liv Spencer

ECW Press

© ECW Press, 2010

Published by ECW Press
2120 Queen Street East, Suite 200, Toronto, Ontario, Canada M4E 1E2
416-694-3348 / info@ecwpress.com

Library and Archives Canada Cataloguing in Publication

Spencer, Liv
    Love bites : the unofficial saga of Twilight / Liv Spencer.

ISBN 978-1-55022-930-1

    1. Meyer, Stephenie, 1973- Twilight saga series--Juvenile literature. 2. Pattinson, Robert, 1986- --Juvenile literature. 3. Stewart, Kristen, 1990- --Juvenile literature. 4. Lautner, Taylor, 1992- --Juvenile literature. 5. Vampires--Juvenile literature. 6. Werewolves--Juvenile literature. 7. Twilight (Motion picture : 2008)--Juvenile literature.

I. Title.

PS3613.E979Z87 2010   813´.6   C2009-905973-8

Text and photo editor: Crissy Boylan
Cover design: Rachel Ironstone
Interior design and typesetting: Tania Craan

Special thank you to Erin Creasey, Jennifer Knoch, Erin Nicole Smith, & Crissy Boylan for their invaluable contributions to this book. You're the Alices to my Bella. Thank you also to the Twilight crafters for participating. — Liv

Second printing, July 2010 at Courier Companies Inc. in the United States of America.

Images Copyright: Barbara Henry/iStock: i, 124, back cover; AP Photo/Matt Sayles: front cover, 1, 29, 43; Jason Lugo/ iStock: 3; Ingo Wagner/dpa/Landov: 4; Christina Radish/Agency Photos: 6, 27, 51, 71, 79, 89, 103, 110, 130, 138, 158, 172, 176; Brian Toro/iStock: 7; BlaneyPhoto/iStock: 9; AP Photo/Elaine Thompson: 10, (Forks sign) 95; Nicholas Roberts/iStock: 11; Tony Nelson/Retna: 12, 91; KingWu/iStock: 14; jimkruger/iStock: 15; brave-carp/iStock: 17; Patrick Lynch/Veer: 20; Brittney McChristy/iStock: 23; Franco Origlia/Getty: 25; Kevin Winter/Getty: 26; Daniel Norman/iStock: 28; Tim Whitby/WireImage: 30; Armando Gallo/Retna: 31, 34, 54, 55, 97, 189; Nathan Shanahan/WireImage: 33; Scot Weiner/Retna: 37; © Summit Entertainment/Supplied by FilmStills.net/Retna: 38, 102, 121, 123; Pixplanete/PR Photos: 41, 190, 201; Chris Ashford/Retna: 44; Henny Garfunkel/Retna: 47; Manny C. Gonzaga/Shooting Star: 49; Sthanlee B. Mirador/Shooting Star: 56, 67, 73, 96, 99, 173, 175; Sue Schneider/MGP Agency: 59, 126, 133, 136, 174; Christian Lapid/Startraksphoto.com: 60; PseudoImage/Shooting Star: 62; Maverick Films/Keystone Press: 65, 87; Sara De Boer/Retna: 77, 80; Sara De Boer/Startraksphoto.com: 85; Albert L. Ortega/WireImage: 93; Natalia Bratslavsky/iStock: (treeline) 95; AP Photo/Jennifer Graylock: 98; Unimedia Europe SND Films © Pe/ADC/Keystone Press: 101; Andrea Staccioli Insidefoto/Photomasi/Retna: 105; RD/Dziekan/Retna Digital: 106; Kevin Mazur/TCA 2009/WireImage: 112; Peter Zelei/iStock: 113, 177; Zack Frank/iStock: 116; xyno/iStock: 119; AP Photo/Chris Pizello: 122; FX. Kushartono/iStock: (wolf) 125; Robert Kenney/Retna: 128; Paul Redmond/ WireImage: 129; miralex/iStock: 131; Yoram Kahana/Shooting Star: 132, 161; AP Photo/Alessandra Tarantino: 134; Frank Micelotta/PictureGroup via AP Images: 137; Allie Henze: 139–43, 162–63, 199, 200; Hedda Gjerpen/iStock: 144; AP Photo/Lefteris Pitarakis: 146; L. Martinez/JpegFoto/PictureGroup via AP Images: 147; Wouter Tolenaars/ iStock: 151; Sergey Rusakov/iStock: 152; Albert Michael/Startraksphoto.com: 157; Rick Egan/ZUMAPress.com/Keystone Press: 159; AP Photo/Marco Ugarte: 160; Robert Smith/Ipa Press/Retna: 165; Alexandra Beier/Getty: 166; Ilia Panfilov/iStock: 169; Dennis Van Tine/Retna: 170; Andrew Hill/iStock: 179; John Spellman/Retna: 186; Mario Anzuoni/Reuters/Landov: 191; Erin Nicole Smith: 193–94, (#2) 196; Nikki Pitcher: (#1) 196; Desiree: (#3) 196; Lisa Kramer-Leggett: (#4) 196; Flor Hernandez: (#5) 196; Paula McDonough: (#6) 196; Heather Ladick: 197; Lester Cohen/WireImage: 203. Decorative backgrounds: iStock.

The publication of *Love Bites: The Unofficial Saga of Twilight* has been generously supported by the Government of Ontario through the Ontario Book Publishing Tax Credit, by the OMDC Book Fund, an initiative of the Ontario Media Development Corporation, and by the Government of Canada through the Canada Book Fund.

Canada

contents

Just a few short years ago, when someone said, "twilight," what came to mind was not sparkling vampires but that magical time of day just before sunrise or after sunset when light scatters beautifully through the atmosphere. The twilight hours have long captured the imaginations of artists, photographers, songwriters, and authors of fiction. But, for Stephenie Meyer and the world of readers she touched with her paranormal romance series, "twilight" would come to mean something else entirely.

Today when someone says, "twilight," so much more comes to mind — a romance between a human girl and an inhumanly beautiful vampire boy; the "near-constant cover of clouds" in Forks, Washington; now-celebrity actors Robert Pattinson, Kristen Stewart, and Taylor Lautner; masses of impassioned fans taking over Comic-Con year after year; and the thick, unmistakable, black-jacketed tomes lining the shelves of bookstores across North America and around the world. The world of the Twilight Saga — the novels, the film adaptations, the actors who bring these beloved characters to life, and the author who started it all — is a rich, complex place celebrated by dedicated, loyal, and involved fans who are in large part responsible for making Twilight the unprecedented success it is. Accepting the British Academy of Film and Television Arts Rising Star award on February 21, 2010, Kristen Stewart thanked the legions of Twilighters who voted for her, who prove "again and again to be the most devoted and attentive fans ever." *Love Bites: The Unofficial Saga of Twilight* was written in the hopes of exploring just what it is that makes us so fiercely attached to Stephenie Meyer's creation.

chapter 1

Stephenie Meyer
Storyteller

Stephenie Meyer may think the "fame thing" is "weird," but as the creator of the Twilight Saga and fictional superstars Bella, Edward, and Jacob, Meyer is something of a rock star herself. In August 2008, to launch *Breaking Dawn*, Meyer added a rock-concert element to her book tour, going on the road with Justin Furstenfeld, frontman of one of her favorite bands, Blue October. On each stop, Meyer took to the stage to answer questions from fans and, as the *LA Times* reported, "ear-piercing screams from the crowd punctuat[ed] the night — seriously, after every sentence, throughout the whole show" it was "as if Meyer was a Jonas Brother."

Who is the woman behind the story that has captivated a passionate, obsessed generation of vampire- and werewolf-lovers? *Time* describes Meyer as "smart, funny, and cheery." She comes across as calm and thoughtful in interviews, and, with her long dark hair falling softly around her face, her appearance is sunny. She explains, "The Goth thing is really not me," and freely admits, that despite having penned a hugely successful supernatural book series, "I'm not really an expert on the subject of vampires. I haven't read many vampire novels — maybe one, but I don't remember its title, and I don't think I have ever seen a vampire movie."

The premise for *Twilight* came to Stephenie in a dream — a dream her millions of fans are grateful she remembered. She explains, "In my dream . . . I can see a young woman in the embrace of a very handsome young man, in a beautiful meadow surrounded by forest, and somehow I know that he is a vampire. In the dream there is a powerful attraction between the two. When I started to write this, I had no idea where it was going; I had no idea at all in the beginning that I was writing a book. I started writing out the scene from my dream [which eventually became chapter 13], and when I got done I was so interested in the characters that I wanted to see what would happen to them next. And so, I just wrote and let whatever happened happen." The thought never occurred to her that what she was working on would eventually be published. "It was just for me, for fun, and I never felt any self-imposed pressure."

At the time, Meyer was 29 years old, and on a typical day had "a million things to do" as she took care of raising her three young sons, Gabe, Seth, and Eli. Her creative pursuits were mostly limited to scrapbooking and making elaborate Halloween costumes. But the morning after her dream she "stayed in bed, thinking about the dream. Unwilling, I eventually got up and did the immediate necessities, and then put everything that I possibly could on the back burner and sat down at the computer to write — something I hadn't done in so long that I wondered why I was bothering."

Reading had always been a favorite escape for Meyer, and even in her early years she delighted in literature through books and scholarly activity. She was born on Christmas Eve in 1973 in Hartford, Connecticut, to Stephen and Candy Morgan. The unusual spelling of her name came when her parents added an "ie" to her dad's name, Stephen. Stephenie says that her status as a Christmas baby has "always given me a bad attitude to birthdays in general." (An attitude she passed on to Bella.)

Stephenie's dad was a CFO for a contracting company, and the family transplanted to Arizona when Stephenie was four. Like Bella, she is fan of the temperate Arizona climate, and considers "temperatures under 75 degrees frigid." The second of six children, she is very close to her family. "I think that coming from such a large family has given me a lot of insight into different personality types — my siblings sometimes crop up as characters in my stories." In fact, she borrowed the names of all of her siblings for characters in the Saga: Emily, Heidi, Paul, Seth, and Jacob.

Stephenie attended Chaparral High School in Scottsdale, Arizona. She was a very shy student who carried on inner dialogues with herself, which probably contributed to her ability to create rich fictional characters. A national merit scholar, she used her award money to help pay for her college education.

She attended Brigham Young University in Provo, Utah (pictured below), where she majored in English.

Around the time that Stephenie's family moved to Arizona, she met Christian "Pancho" Meyer for the first time. While they knew each other as children from church activities — both are Mormon — they didn't really connect until Stephenie was a college student. Pancho was home in Phoenix after completing a mission trip, and Stephenie was visiting her parents on a college break. The two were married nine months later when Stephenie was 21 years old.

Pancho and Stephenie have been married for well over a decade. Since her writing success, Pancho has stopped working as an accountant and is a stay-at-home dad. She admits that her husband and children "all are slightly bewildered with my sudden career

shift from mommy to writer." They live just outside Phoenix, in a large and modern house in Cave Creek. Overzealous fans have managed to track Stephenie down at home — but the Meyer family isn't interested in moving. Stephenie says that phone numbers are easy to change, and she loves her house and how nearby her parents and one of her brothers live.

Meyer is often asked what parts of her personal history she draws from to create her emotional stories, particularly the torturous breakup that Bella suffers in *New Moon*. "I have never suffered a heartbreak like Bella's. Nothing close. The few times I had my heart stepped on, I was not devastated, nor was I melodramatic. Life went on, and I went with it. I was very practical about my rejections, and I was well aware that it was never true love that I was losing. So where does Bella's pain come from? It comes from her. Even if I had experienced the loss of a true love, I know that my reaction would not have been like Bella's. She is a much less cynical person, much more open — to both pain and joy." Meyer often talks about the free will of her characters, how even she doesn't always know what to expect of them: "When writing *New Moon*, at first I didn't know how [Bella] would respond to having her true love taken from her. I was honestly surprised by the way she chose to cope with it."

And has there ever been an Edward in Meyer's life? "No, no, I wish. I've had very typical, normal, human relationships my whole life." She says that her husband thinks that all of the hot male characters in her books are based on him but that he's wrong — if her husband were like Edward, she wouldn't have needed to create Edward in the first place! Still, Pancho does not feel threatened by the fictional characters that inhabit his wife's universe. Meyer says that the character of Carlisle Cullen is much like her own father: they share a strong sense of integrity, and her dad doesn't compromise on his standards. Curiously, her mother-in-law Victoria shares a name with one of the most determined killers in the series!

Meyer had no expectations for her books, and is still overwhelmed by their staggering success. She enthusiastically reports, "I keep getting surprised. When *Twilight* hit the *New York Times* bestseller list at number five, for me that was the pinnacle, that was the moment. I never thought I would be there. And I keep having moments like that where you just stop and say, 'Wait a minute — how is this still going up?' I'm waiting for the rug to be pulled out from under me. I have from day one because I'm kind of a pessimist. But it just keeps being huge." She adds, "I think that after 30 years of being the most normal person in the whole world, it's really hard to become ungrounded. When I'm not out on tour or doing photo shoots, I tend to just forget about it all."

Reading and writing are two pursuits Stephenie closely connects, and holds dear. "A lifelong reader, I didn't start writing until I was 29, but once I began typing I've never been able to stop." Stephenie elaborates, "You live a thousand lives when you read a thousand books." Her favorite books, like *Pride and Prejudice*, the Anne of Green Gables series, along with works by Shakespeare, heavily influence her own work. She is a strong advocate for independent bookstores, and posts book recommendations on stepheniemeyer.com. She also loves C.S. Lewis, Orson Scott Card, and Louisa May Alcott. She encourages her readers to read more, and to ask for advice on what to read from booksellers and librarians: "Ask for guidance, and they will fill your arms with awesomeness!"

Stephenie's work is also influenced by popular and indie music, and she creates playlists to let readers know what she was listening to as she wrote each book. "I listen to music always when I write," she told *Rolling Stone*. "When I hear music on the radio, I'm like, 'Oh! That's a song for this character' or 'This one would so fit that character in this mood!'" One of her favorite bands is Muse — she even dedicated *Breaking Dawn* to them for inspiring her while she was writing. "I spend a lot of time with my characters outside of the book — just letting them live outside the story. When I am in the car, for example, I am often listening to music with my characters in mind."

If she could have a special vampire power, Meyer says: "I think I would just be happy with not having to sleep and not aging. That would be kind of cool." Because her life is so busy, Stephenie does most of her writing at night "often at the sacrifice of sleep" and agrees that her writing habits do fit in well with the vampire theme! She is very open about her process: "Writing done during the day is more likely to be editing rather than the creative kind of effort — it's kind of hard to get into a story when every five seconds you have to get somebody juice or an apple, so anything accomplished during the day was usually rereading and revising." Plus, she adds, "I can't close doors and write. Even if the kids are asleep, I know that I could hear them if I needed. I feel better if I'm kind of in the center of

Stephenie and her husband, Pancho, attend the Hollywood premiere for *The Twilight Saga: New Moon*.

things and I know what's going on."

And for Stephenie, writing is never really finished. "Even today, if I turned to any page in the story, I could probably find at least five words I would want to change, so you never really finish; you just find a good place in the process to quit." Stephenie credits her sister Emily for being her greatest support. "While I was writing, no one except my big sister, Emily, knew that I was actually writing what would eventually turn into a book. She is still my biggest fan and loves everything I write. She read each chapter as I finished it, and she was the one who encouraged me to attempt to get the story published. She is my biggest cheerleader, and I am very grateful to her."

Stephenie can't help but read fan websites and message boards, and she loves interacting with the people who love her books. She is gratified by all of her fan mail but acknowledges: "It's a huge source of guilt. If I could stop time I would sit down and write everyone a three-page letter. There's just no physical way for me to do that, so I feel awful. It's great that people are that excited, but it's hard that I can't

respond." But know that Stephenie takes her readers' comments to heart. "Sometimes the feedback is helpful," she says. "I *want* to be a better writer . . . I read these other authors and I think, 'Now, that's a good writer. I'm never going to reach that level.' But I'm going to be a good storyteller, and what a thing to be!"

She has spent countless hours responding to fan questions — about everything from vampire logistics to the future of Edward, Bella, and Jacob — on her website, on fan forums, and in interviews. She is realistic about the value of her posts and responses to her fans: "People are going to pick apart every line I write for inconsistencies, which of course will exist, because I am not infallible. Sigh."

Stephenie decided to publish *Twilight* because she loved her characters, and she thought that they deserved to be known.

She wanted other people to love the story she dreamed into existence as much as she did. She also believes that writing is what she's meant to be doing with her life. "Writing is now my best escape," she relates. "For me, it's more fulfilling and takes me farther away from the real world than reading does." Along with the Twilight Saga, she has also authored a bestselling science fiction novel, *The Host*. And while she thinks there are definitely more books in her future, she's not yet sure what shape they might take. "People write for different reasons. I have always written to make myself happy. If I'm enjoying a story, feeling the creativity flow, engrossed in a world, then I write and I write fast. If I'm not into it, I can't write. I've never been someone who writes on demand and I can't imagine working that way."

When *USA Today* compared her to J.K. Rowling, whose Harry Potter series similarly took the entertainment world by storm, Meyer said, "There will never be another J.K. Rowling. That's a lot of pressure on me, isn't it?" But she is quick to add, in her characteristically self-assured manner, "I'm just happy being Stephenie Meyer. That's cool enough for me."

She doesn't know why exactly her writing has attracted so much attention: "All I can guess is that when I write, I forget that it's not real. I'm living the story, and I think people can read that sincerity about the characters. They are real to me while I'm writing them, and I think that makes them real to the readers as well." And ultimately, to Stephenie, "Putting words down is where the magic is."

The Dream Comes True

On June 2, 2003, Stephenie Meyer woke up from a dream about a heartbreakingly beautiful boy and a girl in a meadow. The first seed of the epic love story of Edward and Bella was put to paper and the Twilight Saga was born. From a dream to an international phenomenon all within the brief span of four years — how did it all happen?

Meyer says that the story poured out of her. "It gushed. On a good day I would write 10 or 12 pages, single-spaced. That's a good chapter and then some. So it was coming very fast. And then there were other parts that were slower, but it pretty much flowed. I began [*Twilight*] June 2, 2003, and I finished by the end of August."

On a lark, and encouraged by her sister Emily, Meyer got up the nerve to send *Twilight* out to a few literary agents. She went to the

Writer's Market website to look for agents who might be interested in her manuscript, which was simply called "Forks" at the time. After seven or eight rejections, one of the most prestigious literary agents in the U.S., Jodi Reamer of Writers House in New York, took on Stephenie as a client.

Stephenie still wasn't sure exactly what *kind* of book she'd written. "I had a hard time deciding what genre it was exactly, and also for what audience it was written — I really didn't have predetermined ideas about these things, and I don't think it fits exclusively into only certain categories. I actually sent the manuscript out to agents of both adult fiction and young adult fiction. It just so happened that the first agent to invite me into a working agreement was an agent of young adult literature. I was writing it for my 29-year-old self, and I have a sort of fan club of 30-something friends who love the book, so I would say that it is probably appropriate for adults and teen readers, but not too young."

Megan Tingley of the children's division of Little, Brown knew that she had something special in her hands when Reamer, Meyer's agent, presented her with the manuscript. She knew that teenagers were interested in supernatural stories and she was drawn to the romance in Meyer's book. Little, Brown initially offered Meyer $300,000 for a three-book deal. Reamer countered, asking for $1 million, and they eventually settled on an advance of $750,000! A massive sum like that is pretty much unheard of in the book world, especially for a first-time author. "I'd been hoping for $10,000 to pay off my minivan," says Meyer.

Little, Brown's gamble paid off — the books were a massive hit. *Twilight*, released in 2005 with an initial print run of 75,000 copies, was one of the most talked-about novels of the year and extraordinarily popular with its young adult audience. It debuted at number five on the *New York Times* bestseller list. The book received countless awards and accolades, including being an Amazon.com "Best Book of the Decade . . . So Far."

By September 2006, the sequel, *New Moon*, was highly anticipated, and fans crowded bookstores for its release. *New Moon* topped the *New York Times* bestseller list for more than 25 weeks, selling out its initial run of 100,000. The third book, *Eclipse*, launched on August 7, 2007, with a series of midnight parties across North America. The initial print run was one million, and the book sold 150,000 copies in the first 24 hours alone.

Anticipation was at a fever pitch by August 2, 2008, *Breaking Dawn*'s release date. Little, Brown printed 3.7 million copies for the U.S.

Port Angeles, Washington, provides the setting for Edward's second rescue of Bella.

alone, and sold 1.3 million in the first 24 hours. "I kept saying that there will never be another book in my career like *Harry Potter 7*," said Borders' director of children's merchandising, Diane Mangan. "Who would have thought a year later we'd be talking like this again?"

Meyer's Twilight Saga continues to dominate bestseller lists across the globe. In a *Vogue* profile, Meyer was described as "cruising, driving in a fast lane that few authors ever make it to. Meyer has sold a gazillion copies (actual number, 28 million [in English]), so that it sometimes seems as if the interiors of Barnes & Noble are built not with bricks and mortar but with the phone-book-thick volumes of *Twilight*, *New Moon*, *Eclipse*, and, of course, *Breaking Dawn*."

The amazing worldwide phenomenon of the Twilight Saga is an inspiration to writers — and to book publishers. "It just gives you a lot of hope for the future of this business," says Megan Tingley, Meyer's editor. And, along with inspiration and hope, across the globe there is a not-so-quiet buzz of anticipation for whatever Meyer will come up with next.

THE HOST

❋ ❋ ❋

Bored on a drive from Phoenix to Salt Lake City, Stephenie Meyer had another famous dream, but this time, it was a daydream. She told MTV, "I tend to tell myself stories in those situations, and I just caught myself in the middle of this idea about two people sharing a body, both in love with the same guy."

That was the kernel of *The Host*, Stephenie's first foray into adult fiction. The 619-page novel takes readers to a not-so-distant future, when most of the humans on Earth have been colonized by a peaceful yet parasitic species known as Souls who need host bodies to survive, but obliterate the consciousness of their hosts when they take over. A few pockets of uncolonized humans remain, fighting to retain their identities. The novel is told from the perspective of an unusually compassionate old Soul named Wanderer (later nicknamed Wanda), who has previously lived on eight other planets. She is inserted into the body of Melanie Stryder, a former resistance fighter, who appropriately continues to resist Wanderer's presence. Consequently, Wanderer finds herself influenced by Melanie's memories and emotions, feeling them as if they were her own, and goes on a journey to find the two people Melanie loves most: her lover Jared, and her brother, Jamie, who are both still free humans. Wanderer's hunt takes her to a (literally) underground cell of human rebels, who make her their prisoner before slowly accepting her into their community. Living in the underground caves, Wanderer/Melanie is reunited with brooding and passionate Jared, who has trouble accepting his love in a shared body. At the same time Wanderer befriends and comes to love another rebel, the exceptionally warm-hearted Ian, despite Melanie's continued love for Jared. But even as Wanderer lives fairly peacefully underground, a Soul known as The Seeker is looking for the body and Soul that disappeared and, suspecting betrayal, she will not rest until Wanderer is found.

Twilight fans will notice some definite similarities between *The Host* and Stephenie's treasured vampire saga. It's fairly easy to draw parallels between the Jared–Melanie/Wanderer–Ian love triangle and the Edward–Bella–Jacob love triangle. Both Jared and Edward represent unquenchable, undeniable passion, whereas with the Ian and Jacob characters, romantic feelings develop out of friendship. As in the Twiverse, one person risks her existence for the love of another being, even an inhuman one. In *The Host*, Wanderer quickly discovers she wants Melanie to live on, even if it means sacrificing herself. The Cullen clan would approve of Wanderer's blossoming conscience, which causes her to go against the instinct of her species and preserve human lives.

Since it was released, *The Host* has taken up a permanent position on bestseller lists around the world. And though the *Guardian* dismissed it as "little more than a half decent doorstep-sized chunk of light entertainment," most other reviews have been more positive, with *Publishers Weekly* noting it "shines with romantic intrigue," and *Library Journal* asserting "it lives up to the hype, blending science fiction and romance in a way that has never worked so well." Stephenie's already planning a sequel, and has mentioned she could envision the storyline extending to a trilogy.

With the success of the Twilight Saga films, naturally there has been interest in adapting *The Host*, and the rights were bought by Nick Wechsler and Steve and Paula Mae Schwartz. But Stephenie rejected all the script submissions until Andrew Niccol, who penned two of her favorite sci-fi movies, *Gattaca* (which he also directed) and *The Truman Show*, took it on. Speculating on the casting, Stephenie mentioned to MTV that she wanted to switch from casting up-and-comers to more established celebrities, and thought Matt Damon would make a great Jared, and Casey Affleck a good Ian. She may not get her ideal choices, but Stephenie will once again be heavily involved in the process, since producer Nick Wechsler acknowledges the success of the *Twilight* adaptation proves "she knows more about what works than most."

chapter 3

Bella
and Edward
Forever Begins Now

"Bella has a strength, an internal strength,
that makes her very courageous."

– screenwriter Melissa Rosenberg

For some people who have never read a word of Stephenie Meyer's Twilight Saga, its explosive and all-consuming popularity is mystifying. A supernatural romance with vampires who sparkle, werewolves who aren't *actually* werewolves, and a "heroine" so clumsy that her suitors literally carry her everywhere? It's nearly impossible to explain to a non-Twilighter what is so compelling about Meyer's work, primarily because the strengths of her story lie in what, from the outside, seem like its main weaknesses — the choice Bella makes to be with Edward at her own peril, and Bella herself.

The Twilight Saga draws on tales of many star-crossed lovers who came before Bella and Edward — Adam and Eve, Romeo and Juliet, Beauty and the Beast, *Wuthering Heights*' Heathcliff and Catherine, *Pride and Prejudice*'s Mr. Darcy and Elizabeth Bennet. Unlike those love stories, Bella and Edward's romance takes place in the realm of the supernatural and fantastical: as a vampire, Edward's primary instinct is to devour Bella, not to devote himself to loving and protecting her. Can predator and prey be soul mates? Edward's struggle is to resist killing Bella, meanwhile keeping his true identity a secret from the world at large. Trusting a strange, mood-swinging teenage boy is difficult enough in your average human-

human relationship, but Bella Swan has the resolve and determination to put her faith in a vampire — a creature who admits she is to him the sweetest-scented human, like his "own personal brand of heroin." Because both Bella and Edward, individually, are so impossibly drawn to the other, so instantly infatuated, they find staying apart more painful than the difficulties of being together.

In *Twilight*, the intensity of first love — the passion, the awkwardness, the misunderstandings, the perfect moments, the danger of heartbreak — is heightened not only with the threat of violence in a vampiric world but by Bella's first-person narration. Stephenie Meyer positions her reader in the mind of Bella, a girl who "doesn't see herself very clearly," as Edward keenly observes. Like many an adolescent before her, Bella Swan views herself critically and harshly. From her perspective, she's clumsy, withdrawn, boring, and not worth the attention of an average guy like Mike Newton, let alone a god-on-earth like Edward Cullen. That self-judgmental voice is how readers see the *Twilight* universe. Critics have called the writing in *Twilight* emotionally overwrought, the plot slow moving, and the pages spent describing Edward's beauty repetitive and boring. Just as Bella has a hard time paying attention to Jessica when

Explained Stephenie on her website, "The apple on the cover of *Twilight* represents 'forbidden fruit.' . . . The nice thing about the apple is it has so many symbolic roots. You've got the apple in *Snow White*, one bite and you're frozen forever in a state of not-quite-death. . . . Then you have Paris and the golden apple in Greek mythology – look how much trouble *that* started. Apples are quite the versatile fruit. In the end, I love the beautiful simplicity of the picture. To me it says: *choice*."

she dissects the minutiae of her relationship with Mike, readers who don't adopt Bella's perspective when reading the Twilight Saga have a difficult time tolerating her. But *Twilight* is so well loved *because* of Bella's earnestness and unrelenting intensity of emotion. Readers see their own anxieties and insecurities reflected in Bella's, at the same time they experience her fantastical romance as she falls in love with Edward. Bella has also been labeled a bad role model for young girls; she relies on male saviors, her love is obsessive, and she puts her life at risk for a guy, point out the Twihaters. If you looked no further than Bella's interior monologue and trusted it as gospel, it would be easy to come to that conclusion. Bella — who mistakenly thought Edward hated her when they first met, who thinks of herself as a Cowardly Lion but is brave enough to face James alone — may not hold herself in very high regard

"He was really giving me a choice — I was free to refuse, and part of him hoped for that."
Bella (Twilight, 197)

but throughout *Twilight*, her actions reveal a different and more complex character with more agency than even she realizes.

She may be self-conscious and awkward and madly infatuated, but Bella's also the strong, determined, empathetic, and loving girl Edward is helpless but to fall in love with. She is a thoughtful person who sticks to her guns once she makes up her mind about something whether that be moving to Forks, being with Edward, escaping James, or saving her mother from a perceived threat. In interviews and on her website, Stephenie Meyer has emphasized the importance of the theme of choice in *Twilight*. Whether Bella's decisions are right or

wrong, the plot inarguably only progresses with each choice she makes; Bella is very much the key decision-maker in the novel. The world of Forks is opened up to Bella because she chooses to sacrifice her own personal happiness in an effort to make her mother happy. Just as the Cullens make the moral choice to deny their thirst for human blood and live as "vegetarians," Bella knows how to put her own desires aside in support of another — her mother can be with Phil while Bella lands in her own "personal Hell." Navigating Forks High, Bella is polite to her new friends and suitors but never does something unless she wants to. She may be kind but she's not a pushover; she isn't afraid to give firm denials to Mike and Tyler (even if she is chagrined by the attention). With Charlie, Bella shows both her care-giving ability (making him dinner, taking care of the household) as well as her fierce independence. She's very much her father's daughter; though it will take until *Breaking Dawn* for Bella to realize it herself, she has the same qualities of a protector that Charlie has as Forks' police chief, qualities which she admires in both Edward and Jacob.

Besides the obvious, to paraphrase Bella, there's a lot in Edward that Bella is attracted to — perhaps most importantly the similarities they share. Edward has lived over a hundred years hiding his true self from the world, and that guardedness is a quality that Bella has also cultivated in her much shorter life. She hides her feelings in a (failed) effort to go completely unnoticed: she sends her mother "bogusly cheerful emails," she doesn't communicate the strength of her love for Edward at first, and she manages to outplay a psychic and a mood-alterer to escape Alice and Jasper's careful watch over her. Though Edward teases her about her lack of acting skills, Bella is very much a talented actress in the same heartbreaking way that many people are. Feeling that her true self isn't interesting or worth scrutiny and attention, she hides it . . . until she can't help but open up with Edward. Not only do his angelic face and delicious breath make him nearly impossible to resist, but Bella is receptive to Edward because he is curious about her like no one else has ever been. He sees that she is suffering more than she lets on, just as he is, and they both "always say too much" when together. Before they find each other, both Edward and Bella are isolated and lonely, despite the love of their families. Bella immediately identifies with the Cullens, seeing past their impossibly good looks to instinctively recognize that they are just like her: outsiders.

Twilight's epigraph is from the Bible, Genesis 2:17, referencing the famous cursed twosome Adam and Eve: "But of the tree of the knowledge of good and evil, thou shalt not eat of it: for in the day that thou eatest thereof thou shalt surely die." For Edward, Bella is the ultimate "forbidden fruit"; Bella's choice to be with Edward casts her out of the reality she's always known.

> *"'In vain have I struggled. It will not do. My feelings*
> *will not be repressed. You must allow me to tell you how ardently*
> *I admire and love you.' Elizabeth's astonishment was beyond expression.*
> *She stared, coloured, doubted, and was silent."*
>
> *(Pride and Prejudice)*

A loner like her dad, Bella didn't feel like she belonged in Phoenix and feels just as out of place in Forks until she finds a kindred soul in Edward, as well as friendship with (most of) the other Cullens.

After her troubling first encounter with Edward, Bella ruminates on it in a way that she recognizes as obsessive. Knowing her Edward hang-up is "stupid, stupid, stupid," she still can't shake it. What Bella doesn't know in those early days is that he too is battling with his strong feelings for her; if anyone can out-obsess Bella Swan, it's Edward Cullen. Both are also highly emotional people with over-wrought reactions; Bella's manifest inward while Edward's burst out. Over the course of *Twilight*, the push and pull of discovery shapes their relationship and makes them better, stronger, and more complete people — not to mention provides them with the determination to overcome the ruthless James.

Bella has complete faith in the person she loves. She knows Edward's greatest fear — that he will hurt or kill her — will never be realized because of his goodness, his exceptional nature, and his self-control. Her faith in him strengthens him. Edward gives Bella a new perspective on who she is; in his eyes she is the most cap-

tivating and interesting creature in the world. It is no accident that Stephenie Meyer gave her heroine the surname "Swan": as a girl who doesn't recognize her own potential or beauty, Bella embodies "the ugly duckling" tale.

PRIDE AND PREJUDICE

Each novel in the Twilight Saga, says Stephenie Meyer, is inspired by a literary classic. For *Twilight*, Meyer drew from Jane Austen's most celebrated novel *Pride and Prejudice* (1813). Austen's comic romance is centered on Elizabeth Bennet and her unlikely relationship with Mr. Darcy. How they come to fall in love and understand who the other truly is, is the heart of *Pride and Prejudice* and it was this core dynamic that Meyer emulated in shaping her own story.

As in *Twilight*, *Pride and Prejudice* draws its reader in through the point of view of its young female protagonist. (While Austen was a step removed from her heroine using free indirect style — third person narration that enters the thoughts and feelings of its characters freely — Meyer uses first person narration.) Elizabeth Bennet is neither the prettiest girl nor the most accomplished; her mother describes her as "not a bit better than

Edward and Bella connect over their shared love of "Clair de Lune," the third movement from Romantic composer Claude Debussy's *Suite Bergamasque*. Named after a poem by Paul Verlaine, the movement's title means "moonlight," and also references the folk song "Au Clair de la Lune." Debussy (1862–1918) wrote the piece in 1890, but it wasn't published until 1905 — Edward likely first heard it when he was already a vampire.

[her sisters] . . . not half so handsome . . . nor half so good humoured." Like the self-deprecating Bella, Elizabeth is aware of her limitations, of her standing in the pecking order; she would definitely consider herself and Edward to be in seriously different leagues. In Austen's novel, it's not Elizabeth who travels to a new home, but the handsome, wealthy stranger, Mr. Darcy, who visits the small country town where the Bennets live. Mr. Darcy, like Edward, is impossible not to admire but he creates an impression in the townsfolk, and particularly in Elizabeth, of being aloof, standoffish, and too good for them. He is a "fine, tall person, handsome features, noble mien" but has "a most forbidding, disagreeable countenance"; Elizabeth soon decides he is "the proudest, most disagreeable man in the world" and declares his manner is "well bred but not inviting." What she does not realize then is that she has taken a prejudiced view of him; to her, he appears clever, haughty, and reserved — much like Edward does to Bella in her first encounter with him at Forks High School. Neither girl realizes how off those initial impressions will turn out to be.

Just like Bella and her would-be suitor, Elizabeth doesn't know that Darcy has a growing and undeniable admiration for her, despite the differences between them that make a match nearly impossible. There is

MIDNIGHT SUN

In June 2008, Meyer announced that a character study she'd started writing on Edward had turned into the start of a new book – a retelling of *Twilight* from Edward's perspective called *Midnight Sun*. Based on reader feedback, Stephenie realized that Edward was misunderstood, and she offered up the first chapter on her website. Meyer intended to write *Midnight Sun* after *Breaking Dawn*, and the sample chapter ignited fans' unbridled anticipation for another volume in the Twilight Saga.

In August 2008, 12 chapters of the unedited manuscript were leaked to the internet. Meyer said, "I have a good idea of how the leak happened, as there were very few copies of *Midnight Sun* that left my possession, and each was unique." She added she trusts the individual responsible had "no malicious intent." While Meyer was gravely disappointed, she decided to post the chapters on her website, despite her opinion that they were "messy and flawed and full of mistakes." Meyer didn't want her readers "to feel they have to make a sacrifice to stay honest" – and not read an illegal copy elsewhere.

The future of *Midnight Sun* is uncertain. Meyer would still love to see the book published one day, but she's stopped working on it: "*Midnight Sun* is not finished and locked in a safe, waiting for me to be done angsting over the leak. If it were done, I would be throwing it on the bookstore shelves myself. I'd love to be able to give it to all the people who are anxiously waiting for it."

Meyer can't give her fans a prediction about when she'll get back to writing *Midnight Sun*. "I'll get back to *Midnight Sun* when the story is compelling to me again. Just because people want it so badly does not make it more write-able; kind of the opposite, actually. I need to be alone with a story to write, and *Midnight Sun* feels really crowded, if you know what I mean."

Meyer's fans aren't giving up hope that one day *Midnight Sun* will be part of the Twilight Saga collection on their bookshelves. One fan has devoted an entire website, savemidnightsun.com, to convincing Stephenie to bring out the book, and the state of *Midnight Sun* is one of the questions Meyer is most often asked. But for now, Team Edward will have to wait.

something about her that is completely unlike the rest of the women he has met, who tried to win his heart. Like Bella who at first cannot fathom that she could have any significant impact on Edward, Elizabeth doesn't understand that Darcy may be staring at her because he is interested in her; instead of recognizing his attention as admiration, she assumes that

"I can feel what you're feeling now — and you are worth it."
Jasper (Twilight, 404)

there must be something wrong with her — in her dress, her manners, or behavior. Elizabeth is not the only one who finds Darcy's attention to her odd; she has her very own Rosalie in Miss Bingham, a beautiful, rich girl who disapproves of Darcy's affection.

As Darcy realizes "the danger of paying Elizabeth too much attention," he tries the same tactic Edward does — he stays away from her. Luckily for Darcy, Elizabeth doesn't have eyes for her other suitors, just as Bella is not susceptible to the human boys' attempts to woo her. Like Bella not understanding why Mike is so into her when no one paid her any attention in Phoenix, Elizabeth is "more astonished than gratified" by Mr. Collins' interest, and his proposal of marriage strikes her as absurd (just slightly crazier than Mike asking Bella to prom). Just as Jessica and Mike end up getting together, Mr. Collins ends up marrying Elizabeth's friend Charlotte. It is hard for Elizabeth to understand her friend's choice of Mr. Collins; Elizabeth, like Bella, could never settle for a convenient arrangement in marriage — she could only devote herself to someone exceptional.

Austen's heroine and the challenges she faces are mirrored in Meyer's Bella in other ways. Elizabeth observes and evaluates the behavior of the people around her; she's a "studier of character" just like Bella. Watching the other women her age, Elizabeth finds herself removed from the pettiness and trivialities of their interests in the same way that Bella feels distanced from her school friends. Bella becomes braver in the face of James; her literary predecessor Elizabeth's "courage always rises with every attempt to intimidate" her. Elizabeth likes solitude, stealing away for quiet walks and reflection in nature to "indulge in all the delight of unpleasant recollections." Like Bella, Elizabeth replays in her mind what she's said to Darcy, reliving conversations and moments, ruminating on their relationship and its potential. Though her secrets are not quite as universe-altering as "vampires exist and my super hot boyfriend is one," Elizabeth suffers under the weight of concealing the truth from the world around her, dealing alone with Darcy's proposal as well as plot twists concerning Mr. Wickham and Mr. Bingley.

Elizabeth's reaction to Darcy's profession of love is colored by doubt — how could *he* love *her*? It's unbelievable to her, as it is to Bella, that she could produce such strong, undeniable feelings in a man so accomplished. Being in Darcy's presence, especially in front of his sister who she wants to impress, Elizabeth feels an overwhelming array of emotions: awkward, embarrassed, flattered, anxious, and nervous that she will disappoint whom she aims to please. As Bella sees the innate goodness in Edward and the Cullens, Elizabeth comes to recognize the goodness of Darcy's character, his family, and his actions, which at first confused her. Elizabeth's love for Darcy is filled with gratitude that he can

"If I could dream at all,
it would be about you."
Edward (Twilight, 294)

"And so the lion fell in love with the lamb . . ." Though not a direct Biblical quote, the concept of a ferocious lion and a gentle lamb living at peace together is a common Christian symbol of peace on earth, a return to an Edenic paradise that some Christians believe will result from Jesus Christ's return to reign.

love her at all, and continue loving her despite her errors and misjudgments, her faults and misbehavior.

Darcy describes himself as someone who, like Edward, cannot easily converse with strangers; he removes himself from society and appears standoffish when he is simply uncomfortable. When Darcy makes his declaration of love to Elizabeth, he tells her that he has fought desperately against his feelings; she comes to understand that his love for her is "against [his] will, against [his] reason, and even against [his] character" — words that aptly describe Edward's irrepressible love for Bella. Darcy's main character flaw is his obstinacy; not unlike Edward, Darcy's single-mindedness is both frustrating and alluring. Over the course of the novel, Darcy's character grows and changes through his love for Elizabeth. In knowing her, he comes alive to the world and embraces society in a way he resisted before, and there is warmth in his character that develops as he loves Elizabeth. Edward also comes alive through loving Bella; as Alice says to her, "It's been almost a century that Edward's been alone. Now he's found you. You can't see the changes that we see, we who have been with him for so long."

The main reason Bella and Edward seem to be a bad match is rather compelling — his instinct is to kill her — but the subtler reasons are modeled on Darcy and Elizabeth's seeming incompatibility. Darcy is more physically attractive, comes from a higher-class family, and has better "breeding," just as Edward (as a Cullen and a vampire) is more sophisticated, worldly, and traditionally beautiful than Bella. Both Elizabeth and Bella learn that, in the face of true love, these obstacles are meaningless.

From these major themes and characterizations — a relationship "so full of contradictions and varieties" and "moments of such painful confusion" — to smaller echoes — Elizabeth's first visit to Darcy's Pemberley and Bella's to the Cullens' house; a best friend found in her true love's sister — Stephenie Meyer weaves the classic work by Jane Austen into her modern, supernatural romance, creating a richer fabric in *Twilight* and creating legions of new readers of *Pride and Prejudice*.

chapter 4

Adapting Twilight

Stephenie Meyer and Melissa Rosenberg at the afterparty for the *Twilight* premiere on November 17, 2008.

"When I was writing the novel, it was a very visual experience," Stephenie Meyer said of *Twilight*. "I really wanted to see it brought to life." After a somewhat infamous first false start to turn *Twilight* the novel into *Twilight* the film (with Bella remodeled as a sporty, upbeat girl), Meyer knew that not every movie company or screenwriter would honor her vision. With the film rights back up for grabs, Summit Entertainment entered the picture and convinced the author of their love and respect for the original material. Showing more understanding for the medium of film than many novelists, Meyer said, "I knew [the book was] too long to be a movie, some things don't translate visually — it's going to have to change. But some things — the Cullens all have to be in existence, Bella has to be 17, she has to be a clumsy girl with a single dad and a mom living somewhere else. . . . All these basic bones of who these people are have to be in existence. . . . It was really reassuring to me that they [Summit] were happy — eager — to say yes, of course, we want it to be like the book."

The person assigned the unenviable task of taking a beloved work of fiction and translating it into a screenplay was Melissa Rosenberg. A writer for television (*Party of Five, Ally McBeal, The O.C.*) and film (*Step Up*), Rosenberg was in the thick of writing and producing Showtime's serial-killer series *Dexter* when the opportunity to work on *Twilight* arose. Guessing correctly that adapting the novel would mean the already busy woman would "have no life," she nevertheless jumped at the chance. Just as Stephenie Meyer wrote the novel in a short time span, Melissa Rosenberg found herself with little time to translate *Twilight* from page to screen: "The first draft of *Twilight* took five weeks because that was all I had due to the [2007–2008 Writers Guild of America] strike. It was insane. Crazy fast writing." She consulted with Meyer during the process, a relationship that was tentative at first: "When we first started I was much more protective because I didn't know her and she didn't know me. But when we met she realized I was only about respecting her work and I realized she was only about respecting my creative process." Rosenberg not only had to make an author and a studio happy, she had the Twilighters to keep in mind

Director Catherine Hardwicke's vision and enthusiasm ensured the film adaptation of *Twilight* would be a success.

too. "There's a great deal of pressure knowing how important this is to the fans. How personally they take it," admitted Rosenberg. Pushing that anxiety aside, Rosenberg decided she was "just going to have to trust that we

To draw viewers into Bella's world, Rosenberg sparingly used voiceover narration: "A little bit in the beginning, and then the end. . . . Almost all of it is directly from the book, so that helps keep alive the tone of the book."

really were true to the book and that if things aren't specifically in the movie at least the soul and emotion of the book will be translated."

Helping Rosenberg adapt *Twilight*, a story very much grounded in the interior life of Bella, to the visual medium of film was Catherine Hardwicke. The director of *Thirteen* (2003) and *Lords of Dogtown* (2005) got her start as an architect before moving into production design — a strong visually focused background which would result in her rich onscreen look for *Twilight*. Hardwicke calls the source material "such a cool book," and

wanted to make it come alive, to "lift it off the page into a thrilling experience." Like Rosenberg, Hardwicke was very aware that there was a fandom to please but when it came to the daily grind of filming, that pressure pushed her crew to be their best. "It helped in a way because when you'd be up there on top of a mountain freezing in the middle of the night, and then you'd see *Twilight* fans there; it's like, 'Okay, these people care, man. I've got to do it great.' So in a way, it's, like, helpful. It lifts us up and gets us excited that you guys are excited."

But before Catherine Hardwicke and her crew were on location in and around Portland, Oregon, filming this epic love story, she and her casting department had to find the perfect actors to bring these beloved characters to life. It was no easy feat to find Bella Swan and Edward Cullen among mere mortals, but after a grueling search the cast of *Twilight* was assembled.

chapter 5

Robert Pattinson as Edward Cullen

get-up, he didn't look "devastatingly inhumanly beautiful." Rob admits, "I looked like somebody beat me in the face. I was wearing this disgusting wig, and they were like, 'This is Edward.'" But it's a testament to the young actor's talent, charisma, and dedication, that in no time, RPattz haters became lovers, and he has become the definitive Edward Cullen.

Robert Thomas Pattinson was born on May 13, 1986, to Clare, a modeling scout, and Richard, a vintage car importer. He was raised in the posh Barnes area of London, England, with his two older sisters, Victoria and Lizzie, who were fond of dressing young Robert up as a girl and introducing him to people as "Claudia." Like her younger brother, Lizzie was headed for a life in the limelight. At 17, the singer-songwriter was discovered by an EMI talent scout, and she went on to tour and record with electronica group Aurora, earning two top 20 hits, and playing before massive European audiences. Lizzie also collaborated with house DJs/producers Milk & Sugar, and their song "Let the Sun Shine" topped the Billboard Dance Chart.

Robert shares his older sister's love of music, taking up the piano at a young age. Music also provided his first career ambition. He told *People*, "When I was young I wanted to play the piano in a bar, to be the old dude with a whiskey glass, all disheveled." Robert also developed his artistic side at the Tower House School in London, a preparatory school for boys aged 4–13 with a strong arts curriculum. And though Robert's artistic side may have flourished at Tower House, he was not a stellar student and, according to a 1998 school newsletter, was "a runaway winner of last term's Form Three

Though just a glimpse of him now sends his admirers into ecstasies of delight, when he was first cast as Edward, Robert Pattinson was vehemently rejected by the *Twilight* community. An online petition to have him replaced collected 75,000 signatures, and bloggers called him "repulsive" and a "gargoyle." Certainly in some photos of him in a Viking

untidy desk award." It wasn't just disorganized papers though, as his aunt told *US*, "He was hopelessly lazy!" (Rob didn't grow out of his sloppiness — he admitted during an interview with the *Guardian* from a Vancouver hotel room,

"I don't let the maids in. I don't even pull the duvet down now because I don't want to see what's underneath.")

The unruly youngster got his first exposure to the stage while at Tower School, appearing in school productions such as an adaptation of William Golding's *Lord of the Flies*. Robert left Tower House at age 12, when he enrolled in the Harrodian School. The change in school didn't really improve his performance though, and the less-than-stellar student recalls, "I moved to a mixed [gender] school and then I became cool and discovered hair gel."

Robert's newly gelled coif wasn't just getting attention at school; at his mother's encouragement Robert also did some modeling. He explained, "I got lots of jobs, because it was during that period where the androgynous look was cool. Then, I guess, I became too much of a guy, so I never got any more jobs." Looks like his time as "Claudia" was good training for his modeling career! Now the actor looks back on those days with a tinge of embarrassment. "There are so many photos from that time where I look unbearably awkward. I'd just be looking in random directions and stuff."

Modeling clearly wasn't for Robert, but luckily around the same time, he found a different extra-curricular that suited him better in the Barnes Theatre Group. Typical of a 12-year-old boy, he didn't take up drama out of artistic ambition: "I only went to drama class because when I was young I was in a restaurant with my dad and he met this bunch of pretty girls who said that's where they were going!" Little did Rob know, acting would soon lead him to more female attention than he could handle.

Even if it was girls that got him to Barnes, it was his talent that kept him there. Robert's first role was a small part as a Cuban dancer in *Guys and Dolls*. The aspiring actor soon worked

his way up to a more prominent role, as the villainous Alec in *Tess of the d'Urbervilles* — a performance that caught the attention of an agent. Looking back, Robert recognizes the pivotal part Barnes played in launching his career, saying, "I owe everything to that little club."

The agent helped Rob get his first film role playing Reese Witherspoon's son in the 2004 Mira Nair feature film, *Vanity Fair*. Unfortunately, Rob's first performance wouldn't actually make it to theaters: something the actor didn't know until he attended the screening. Rob recounted the *Vanity Fair* debacle to *Vanity Fair* magazine: "[Tom Sturridge] and I . . . we had scenes right next to each other and it was both our first jobs. . . . We went to the screening, and we thought the whole thing was such a joke anyway, because we had no idea what we were doing. We were, like, 'acting' or whatever — we had no idea — and we watched [Tom's] scene and were like, 'Yeah, that's pretty good, that's all right.'" But Robert failed to make his big screen debut. "I'm sitting there going, 'Ummm . . . really?' No one had told me that I had been cut out." The actor is notoriously critical of his own performances (he walked out of *Twilight* a third of the way through), so it may have been his most relaxing film to watch. For those who don't want to miss Rob in period costume, his scene was restored from the cutting-room floor for the DVD.

Rob *could* be seen that year in the made-for-TV Viking saga *Ring of the Nibelungs*, which recounts the adventures of Siegfried the dragon slayer. In the U.K. the film had a theatrical release, but it was the German-language version that was a big hit; the two-part special earned stellar ratings on German TV. The most

Rob at the premiere of *Harry Potter and the Goblet of Fire* with Emma Watson (left) and Katie Leung (right) in 2005.

lasting impact the movie would have on Rob's career is the photos of him in Viking garb, which were used as ammunition against his casting as Edward Cullen.

Despite his disappointment about *Vanity Fair*, the incident turned out to have a serious silver lining. The casting agent felt guilty for not telling Robert about the cut, and suggested the actor when casting began for Hogwarts wonderkid Cedric Diggory in the fourth installment of the Harry Potter series. It was a perfect fit, and *Goblet of Fire* director Mike Newell explained, "Robert Pattinson was born to play the role; he's quintessentially English with chiseled public schoolboy good looks."

Harry Potter and the Goblet of Fire turned out

to be the highest-grossing film of 2005, earning over $895 million in international box office receipts. The success of the film thrust Robert into the spotlight, and he admits he didn't always handle his success well. Looking back, he remarked, "I've changed so much. I'm not nearly as cocky as I was. I was a real prat for the first month. I didn't talk to anyone." Of course, he had reason to be a little cocky, as British newspapers identified him as one to watch, and he was declared "the next Jude Law."

His earnings from the film allowed Robert to move out into his own apartment, but despite the media attention, roles didn't pour in. He was cast in the West End production of *The Woman Before*, but his odd performance got him sacked before opening night. The actor chalks it up to inexperience, saying, "I think I just got confused, doing random mannerisms, as if that made an interesting performance." Rob's earlier soaring confidence proved fleeting, and he suddenly became more self-conscious about his abilities. "I specifically hadn't done anything which anyone would see since *Harry Potter* because I wanted to teach myself how to act. I didn't want to be an idiot," he explained.

The actor couldn't land a job, and eventually he just started ignoring his agent's calls, considering giving up acting altogether. He focused instead on his music. Robert's musical abilities had progressed since he was a boy dreaming of being a whiskey-soaked pianist. He learned to play classical guitar at age five and also took a brief foray into rap in his early teens, confiding that, at age 14, he was part of a rap trio that was "pretty hardcore for three private school kids from suburban London." They may have thought they were hardcore

> "Some guys are pretty but not dangerous. Other guys are dangerous but they're not pretty enough. . . . [Rob Pattinson]'s got both sides."
> – Stephenie Meyer

but, Pattinson adds, "my mum's, like, cramping our style, popping her head in to ask, 'You boys want a sandwich?'" Robert abandoned his dreams of rap glory, and focused instead on guitar and singing, influenced by legendary artists like Van Morrison and Jeff Buckley. Rob started performing alone or with a friend or two at open mic nights . . . where no one really paid attention to him. But just a few years later, people would pay much more attention to the actor's musical talents, especially after Catherine Hardwicke put two of Robert's songs, "Never Think" and "Let Me Sign," in *Twilight*. "One of my favorite parts of making the movie," she told the *LA Times*, "was watching Rob play the music he wrote. He just lets it out, and it breaks your heart." Music remains Robert's back-up career plan; he stresses, "Music occupies a very important place in my life. I couldn't live without music."

When he did decide to go back to the acting world, Robert's next few projects were appropriately low profile. He starred as Toby Jugg, a wheelchair-bound Royal Air Force pilot, in the psychological thriller *The Haunted Airman*, which aired on the BBC. The reviewer in *The Stage* couldn't help but comment that the star's "jawline is so finely chiseled it could split granite," but went on to praise Robert's portrayal of the pilot with "a perfect combination of youthful terror and world weary cynicism." Robert followed that performance with a role in another TV project, *The Bad Mother's Handbook*, which aired in 2007.

Two feature films followed these TV movies. In indie dramedy *How to Be*, Rob continued his streak of playing what he calls "weirdos," as Art, a down-on-his-luck 20-something who has to move in with his parents. But unlike most 20-somethings who return to parental rule, Art invites a self-help expert to live with him, in hopes it will help him get his life back on track. Director Oliver Irving picked Britain's near-forgotten golden boy because he "had a uniqueness and unpretentiousness. A lot of people who had come from drama school . . . were trying to fit into a kind of dramatic mold. He was a lot more relaxed. Just kind of came and was willing to make a mistake and laugh at himself." The film was a success on the festival circuit, and Rob earned the Best Actor prize at the Strasbourg Film Festival, and the film took home the Audience Award in New Orleans. *How to Be* also gave Robert an opportunity to showcase his musical talent, when he was featured on a soundtrack for the first time. Rob can be heard singing "Chokin' on the Dust" (Parts 1 and 2) and "Doin' Fine."

After *How to Be*, Robert went from demonstrating his own artistic side to capturing someone else's when he was cast in his most challenging role yet, as famous surrealist painter Salvador Dali in the indie drama *Little Ashes*. The film explores Dali's formative years as a young man at the University in Madrid, and his complicated relationship with poet Federico García Lorca. It was a demanding role, and Robert gave himself over to it completely. He explained, "It was the first job I had where I had an opportunity to obsess over something." This obsession extended to reading the painter's autobiographies and studying photographs of him. "I just researched tons and tons of stuff because everyone spoke Spanish on the set and so I just read all day. It was the first time that I ever really got into characterization, trying to work on movements. There was a photo of him pointing and I kept trying to figure out how he pointed for, like, three days. I've never done that for any job. I was doing tons of stuff on his walk and such," said Rob. Ultimately, that led Rob to really connect with the conflicted artist. "I've never related to a character more than him," he admits, "which is really weird because everyone thinks that he's some nut job." *Little Ashes* had a limited release in 2009, garnering mixed reviews, though the small film got huge attention from all-things-Pattinson being newsworthy.

But before superstardom hit, Robert was just another out-of-work actor, who had never heard of the *Twilight* books. He did hear about the casting call for Edward, and even went so far as to make an audition tape, but "it looked so ridiculous I didn't even send it," and he put the whole thing behind him. After reviewing around 5,000 tapes, Catherine Hardwicke and the Summit Team still hadn't found their lead vampire. Summit exec Erik Feig had a colleague take a closer look at British actors, even lesser-known ones, and print out headshots. Pulled because of his *Harry Potter* role, the Summit team loved his look, but Catherine Hardwicke remained skeptical: could this Byronic Brit actually pull it off?

Robert paid for his own flight out to L.A., sleeping on his agent's couch before the audition. Most actors had been portraying Edward as the perfect creature Bella sees, but Robert wanted to find a difficult angle. "I tried to emphasize the danger and make the more gentlemanly side of this character a veil to something else underneath. I really tried to make him an incredibly strong and powerful character, but at the same time self-loathing and extremely vulnerable," explains Rob.

Rob was still burdened by the insecurities of a year of no work, and was nervous approaching the audition — especially since it would involve a love scene with Kristen Stewart. The day of his audition he notoriously took part of a valium to calm himself down, though his actual audition (which was held at Hardwicke's house) was anything but calm. He threw himself around, banged his head against the wall, fell off the bed, and unleashed the primal side of the otherwise gentlemanly Edward Cullen.

Catherine and Kristen were auditioning the four top contenders that day, and for both director and actress, Rob left the competition behind. Kristen remembers, "Everyone came in playing Edward as this happy-go-lucky guy. . . . But I got hardcore pain from Rob. It was purely just connection." Hardwicke elaborates, "I was looking to see who really had that magic, who had that chemistry. Rob and Kristen had it from the first day."

Robert saw it differently: he was sure he'd blown the audition. He related to *Vanity Fair*, "I remember calling my parents [afterward] and saying, 'That's it. I'm not doing this anymore.' And then hearing, 'Okay, fine,' which was not the answer I wanted to hear at all."

But shortly after, Robert did get an answer he wanted to hear: he would be playing Edward Cullen. He immediately launched into researching the role, his fervor similar to the one he felt learning about Dali. Since the filmmakers said they wanted to revamp the vampire genre, the would-be Edward didn't bother watching old vampire flicks ("I saw the original *Nosferatu*, but he definitely isn't dating material," jokes Rob). He read the three existing *Twilight* books in one weekend following his screen test, and two-thirds of the unpublished *Midnight Sun* manuscript, courtesy of Stephenie Meyer. Trying to experience the boredom and isolation of Edward, Robert contemplated not speaking to anyone for a month, although this proved to be a little too extreme. He did write journal entries as Edward, trying to get into the tortured vamp's mindset.

And though much has been made of Taylor Lautner's transformation for *New Moon*, Robert also had to whip himself into shape before he appeared in front of the camera. He told *The Times of India*, "Before *Twilight*, I never worried much about exercising my abs out, but for being Edward, I did every freaking thing possible. Regularly for two to three months, I ran for two hours daily and had a three-hour long session of kickboxing followed by hitting the gym for some weight training and abdomen crunches. In addition, I was on a stringent diet regime too. I was just trying to lose every ounce of body fat, so when I took off my shirt, I would look like an alien." Despite his dedication, Rob never blew up to Lautner-esque proportions, and he admits, "It didn't really work out."

Once filming began, Robert worked to humanize Edward, seeing him not as a vampire, but as "a normal guy who got bitten by someone." Sometimes the actor pushed his tortured soul interpretation too far. Looking back, Robert has since realized, that in creating the perfect man, "you wouldn't write him as some manic depressive weirdo who's trying to kill himself all the time — whatever his six pack is like. So I spent a long time fighting with producers. Catherine got me a copy of the book with every instance that he smiled highlighted and I was just like, 'Okay, fine.'"

Although Rob wasn't Stephenie Meyer's first choice to play her dazzling hero — she favored Brit Henry Cavill (*The Tudors, Tristan + Isolde*), who was too old to play Edward by the time the film was being made — she quickly warmed to Robert on her visits to the set. She remarked that the chemistry between Kristen and Robert "may cause hyperventilation," and praised Robert's performance as "Oscar worthy."

After the movie opened and shattered everyone's expectations for the project, both of Stephenie Meyer's assessments proved bang on. Twilighters everywhere could attest to the potential for hyperventilation, and while Robert wasn't awarded the little gold man, he did participate in the 2008 Oscar ceremony. Though the Academy rarely gives attention to teen films or "commercial" projects, Robert found himself sitting in the audience among Hollywood legends, and on stage with Amanda Seyfried, introducing a montage of love scenes that featured clips from *Twilight*. For Robert, it was an experience more surreal than playing Dali: "I got there and I'm sitting in the second row. To think back to the year before . . . it's unbelievable."

About his performance, Robert remains modest. He won an MTV Movie Award, Teen Choice Award, and Scream Award for best actor, but he still attributes his success to his oft-discussed hair. "In a lot of ways the hair is 75 percent of my performance," he quips. As the movies progress, you'll notice his hair gets more relaxed, though when a hair fell out of place during one sequence in *New Moon*, panic ensued on set. "There were about five people in five different departments who, because of my forelock, ended up in tears," he told *Entertainment Weekly*.

His co-stars who have gotten to know this self-effacing star are a little dismayed about the attention paid to his unruly mane or his physique, rather than the man himself. "He's really talented, he's really smart, he's really musical, he's an intellectual, he reads," said vamp sib Nikki Reed. "That's the side that I wish people would [ask about]. I don't know if anyone necessarily even knows him . . . that side of him." Having endured a similar onslaught of attention from fans and media alike, Kristen is impressed with how Rob has handled his newfound celebrity. She noted, "I've seen him grow a lot, and I've seen him get more comfortable with his position [as a celebrity]. But I also don't see any change in who he is."

The hotly desired heartthrob admitted he's not really interested in changing, in giving up the life he has for one of fame and fortune. He told *Harper's Bazaar*, "I don't spend any money. The only thing I've really bought is my car, which cost $1,500 and keeps exploding. It would be nice to buy a house for my parents, but at the same time my parents are so comfortable where they live; they would probably just feel like it was a burden. I wear the same clothes every day and the only thing I used to splurge on was DVDs." Just like he's not waylaid by a lavish lifestyle, the actor still hangs on to his old friends, valuing their opinion above all else: "The only people that I try to impress are my little group of friends . . . I've

kind of grown up around really competitive, artistic-type people, and I'm very, very grateful for that."

And even though all his public appearances are accompanied by screaming choruses of frenzied female fans, Robert still considers himself a rough-edged Romeo. He told *Seventeen*, "I never get asked out on dates. And I never know how to go about asking people. I'm not good at the whole 'dinner' thing. I'm a bit of a loner." He playfully dodges any serious questions about his love life, especially if it involves rumors about a romantic relationship with his leading lady. Asked how he approached kissing scenes in the movie, the actor joked, "I kinda just approached it from the front."

After years of struggling, Robert finally has his choice of parts, but he is well aware that being a "bankable" actor comes with tremendous responsibility. He explains, "It's definitely different because you get offered stuff you'd never have dreamed of getting offered before. But it's scary as well because you don't have to audition for anything. I don't want to do a movie just so it gets made." Other than *Twilight* sequels, so far only a couple of films have passed Rob's quality control. In *Remember Me*, Robert plays Tyler Roth, a young privileged NYU student who is able to escape his own family tragedy when he meets Ally Craig (*Lost*'s Emilie de Ravin). Director Allen Coulter was impressed with Robert's dedication to the project, saying, "[Robert]'s so obsessed about delivering a performance he feels happy with that he is constantly watching the dailies. He's religious about it." After *Remember Me*, the actor has very different projects lined up. He's been cast as kidnapped son Phineas in the western *Unbound Captives* (with Rachel Weisz and Hugh Jackman) and is also slated to appear in historical drama *Bel Ami*, where he'll play "totally amoral" manipulative journalist Georges Duroy opposite Uma Thurman and Kristen Scott Thomas. In *Circus*, Rob falls for Reese Witherspoon's character in the adaptation of Sara Gruen's novel *Water for Elephants*.

These diverse roles are a testament to Robert's tremendous talent and dramatic range, although for thousands of RPattz fans around the world, he'll always be remembered as chivalrous and loyal Edward. At times he may even be mistaken for his character, who he calls, "the hero of the story that just refuses to accept that he's the hero," adding, "I think that's kind of admirable." And Twilighters everywhere feel the same way about him.

chapter 6

Kristen Stewart as Bella Swan

Kristen doesn't feel like she's changed much since she was a little kid. (Pictured here at the *Panic Room* premiere in 2002.) "Think about when you were five years old. Don't you feel like you're the same person now? Like you were fundamentally who you are when you were a little kid? We are who we are at five."

She stumbles, she fidgets, she restarts sentences halfway through or abandons them altogether. She doesn't perk up for the media, won't tap dance through an interview, and was almost uniformly trashed for "bombing" *The Late Show with David Letterman.* She's been called aloof or just plain snobby. But for Kristen Jaymes Stewart, this is all part of Sean Penn's apt description of her as "a truth machine."

Kristen prefers to act on movie sets only and just tries to keep it real by honestly presenting herself to the world — take it or leave it. She doesn't dress like a celebrity ("People think that I'm a really terrible dresser. But I don't dress for fashion magazines. I dress like a normal person," she told *Allure*), and in interviews she doesn't plaster on a smile and raise her voice an octave. But that doesn't mean she doesn't care about her projects — nothing could be further from the truth. Her guardedness comes from her loyalty to her projects. She explained, "I spend so much time guarding against sounding insincere about something that I would die for. Maybe I'm overcompensating. . . . I care so much. And it gets reported as the opposite."

Of course Kristen didn't go into show business completely oblivious to the demands of stardom. She was born April 9, 1990, in Los Angeles, California, into a Hollywood family. Though there aren't any other actors, her mother, Jules Mann-Stewart, is a longtime script supervisor, and recently a writer and director. Her father, John Stewart, is a stage manager and television producer. Her older brother Cameron also joined the family business, working as a film grip (an on-set technician who rigs cameras and lighting).

Kristen got to experience "Take Your Kid to Work" day all the time, and told *People*, "I was really comfortable on movie sets. I would go on location with my mom sometimes." The L.A. native always admired her parents' work: "I was always really proud to go to school and say, 'My parents make movies.' It was just the family job."

It was only a matter of time before Kristen was reeled in. She didn't get pulled into acting because of family connections: she was discovered. She was singing the Dreidel song at a Christmas concert when she was eight, and an agent recognized her talent. "I still don't remember saying 'Yeah,' but I remember thinking that I could totally do it," says Kristen.

She was right, but even as someone who grew up on the film scene, it wasn't easy to break in. She auditioned for a year before she got her first role. "It took a really long time until I was totally over it and then came my last audition. I went to it and I didn't even want to. My mum said: 'Well, this is the last one. You don't have to go to any more.' And that was the first movie I got," recalls Kristen. The role that altered Kristen's path was as a girl waiting for water in the Disney made-for-TV movie *The Thirteenth Year*. She was cast in another uncredited non-speaking role as a ring-toss girl in *The Flintstones in Viva Rock Vegas*.

In 2001's *The Safety of Objects*, Kristen finally got to speak onscreen. She played the tomboy daughter of Patricia Clarkson's character in the independent drama that follows several different suburban families, ultimately revealing the connections between their lives. The film got her some attention, as she told

"Kristen's a very serious actor and she has a lot of experience. And it was excellent to have someone like that at the center of things. Bella's a hard role to take on because this is a first-person novel. The people who're reading it, for the time that they're reading it, they're Bella and so you don't have this other person between you and the story."

– Stephenie Meyer

Interview, "I know that when I did *The Safety of Objects*, everybody was like, 'Oh, this kid is so confident; she's such a little star.' But I never wanted to be the center of attention — I wasn't that I-want-to-be-famous, I-want-to-be-an-actor kid."

Though *The Safety of Objects* was an important career milestone, it was her role as the diabetic daughter of Jodie Foster in the 2002 thriller *Panic Room* that distinguished her as an actress to watch. Along with a boost to her popularity, working with the talented and well-established Jodie Foster was a tremendous learning experience for Kristen. "Watching Jodie shaped my ideas about how an actor should behave on set," said Kristen. "She's very professional. She's there to do the job." Foster would become Kristen's career role model, since, Kristen notes, "She's not just an actress — she's a director, she's a producer, she's a writer." The Academy Award–winning actress hasn't forgotten her young protégé either, and has watched her develop as an actress: "Kristen isn't interested in blurting out her emotions all in front of her, and that results in really intelligent and interesting performances." High praise coming from such a celebrated and successful actress. Critics agreed with her, and Kristen was nominated for a Young Artist Award for *Panic Room*.

As Kristen's career picked up speed, her academic performance suffered, and she ended up leaving regular school in favor of correspondence during the seventh grade. The actress explained, "When I would go away to work, my teachers would only give me a portion of my schoolwork, and then I'd come home and they'd fail me. I made too much work for them. . . . I was very happy to leave." As determined then to be herself as she is now, Kristen also had trouble fitting in with the other kids. "If you didn't wear the right pair of jeans — and I was so not that kid — then you were totally scrutinized and persecuted," she told *Nylon*. Leaving school also clarified her existing relationships: "When I stopped going to school, I got the strongest dose of perspective. . . . I lost all my friends but the few that were really close to me. And I still maintain those friendships."

Now Kristen had more time to act, and she continued building her résumé. She worked alongside more powerhouse actors like Dennis Quaid and Sharon Stone in the 2003 psychological thriller *Cold Creek Manor*, playing Kristen Tilson, the daughter in a family that moves to a country estate with a dark past. The film was generally panned; though the *New York Times* called it "scream-by-numbers," the reviewer noted the somewhat redeeming influence of a "stellar cast."

In August 2003, Stewart started work on Showtime original movie *Speak*, an adaptation of the novel by Laurie Halse Anderson, which tells the story of Melinda Sordino, a 13-year-old who is raped by an upperclassman, and is so traumatized that she stops speaking entirely. The *New York Times* reviewer highlighted Kristen's performance, saying she "creates a convincing character full of pain and turmoil — not an easy acting feat, since because of the nature of the story she has a limited number of lines." It would be the first of many dark roles for Stewart, but those are the roles that come naturally to her: "When I have to laugh and be happy in a scene, it kind of freaks me out. If I have to have a breakdown or get all emotional, that's easy." Playing victimized Melinda Sordino ignited the acting spark in Kristen, and she remembers, "It was the first time I lived through something from another person's perspective. It felt like I changed." Something changed in Kristen's personal life as well, since it was on that set that she would meet long-time boyfriend Michael Angarano (*Almost Famous*, *Lords of Dogtown*, *Will & Grace*).

Kristen landed her first lead role in a feature film in the light-hearted heist flick *Catch That Kid!* (with Max Thieriot and Corbin Bleu). She also returned to thrillers in 2004's *Undertow*, about two brothers fleeing their murderous uncle. In 2005, Kristen got a chance to work with successful director Jon Favreau (*Iron Man*, *Elf*) in *Zathura*, another board-game-gone-wild fantasy/adventure in the style of *Jumanji*. Kristen plays the older sis to two younger brothers, who start playing a board game and end up hurtling through space.

Unfortunately, the movie underperformed at the box office, partially because of some unbeatable competition from Kristen's future *Twilight* co-star's *Harry Potter and the Goblet of Fire*. The same year Kristen also appeared in the drama *Fierce People* about a down-and-out mother and son who move from New York to a rich country estate, where they discover the country club circuit can be as fraught with peril as the Lower East Side. The movie had a limited release and garnered mixed reviews.

Kristen continued to see-saw between indie films and bigger budget studio productions, a strategy used by Ms. Foster herself, who noted, "It allows her not to get stuck with the shelf-life problem." Kristen's next film, indie drama *In the Land of Women*, debuted at the Cannes Film Festival in 2006, though it wasn't shown in theaters until April 2007. Kristen stars opposite Meg Ryan, who plays her dying mother, and *The O.C.*'s Adam Brody, who plays a friend from across the street and her mother's secret love interest. As with all her roles, Kristen found something relatable in her role as Lucy: "My character was really trying to fit in. And she realizes that she doesn't have to, that she's awesome in her own right. That's the most self-conscious part I've played in my life. Literally in every scene, all you see are my hands in my hair and me biting my lips and nails."

In 2007 Kristen's first appearance on the big screen was in *The Messengers*, directed by the Pang brothers, about an unremarkable sunflower farm invaded by a dark force, which turns the farm's inhabitants on one another. Drawn to the story and the renowned Pang brothers, Kristen enjoyed playing daughter Jess

At Sundance to promote *Speak* in January 2004. Kristen met boyfriend-to-be Michael Angarano on that film: "I never thought I would date an actor, but he's my best friend."

Solomon: "She's really a desperate character and it's nice because she really triumphs. It's nice when you can see a young, teenage girl actually get up and kick butt and empower herself."

The actress returned to the indie film scene for one of her most challenging roles yet, playing a young woman with Friedreich's ataxia in *The Cake Eaters* (2007). Friedreich's ataxia is an incurable degenerative nerve disorder, and Kristen's character, Georgia Kaminski, is determined to be independent and experience love before she's wheelchair-bound. Wanting to do the character justice, Kristen got to know some young women living with the disease, and says, "They are so unbelievably brave and honest. . . . They are willing to enjoy life, while everyone around them just wants to pity them." She calls it "an optimistic, triumphant story." The film premiered at the Tribeca Film Festival, doing the indie circuit with a limited theatrical release in 2009. Reception of the film was fairly good, and Kristen's performance was widely praised. The *New York Times* noted, "Ms. Stewart's tough, strong performance avoids sentimentality to such a degree that her character isn't even particularly likable. But as she schemes to get what she wants come hell or high water, you cheer her on."

Kristen continued to find a balance between big-ticket appeal and indie integrity with the adventure/drama *Into the Wild* (2007), an adaptation of Jon Krakauer's bestselling chronicle of the tragic journey to Alaska of free-spirited Christopher McCandless. Kristen plays a girl with a crush on the protagonist; her scenes may be relatively brief but her performance was memorable. The film gave Kristen an opportunity to work with Sean Penn, who wrote and directed the film. Penn was impressed with the young actress, calling her "magically easy to direct," and adding, "She is a real force with terrific instincts." And while Penn praised her acting, co-star Emile Hirsch praised the actress herself, saying: "She's not a pushover. She's really strong and fun to hang out with." The film was a huge success, receiving enthusiastic reviews, winning numerous awards, and earning a spot on various year-end top 10 lists, including those of the American Film Institute and the National Board of Review. Much of the praise was for the leading man, but renowned critic Roger Ebert sagely noticed Kristen's performance, predicting, "Here is an actress ready to do important things."

Kristen rounded out 2007 by appearing in her first short film, *Cutlass*, which was actress Kate Hudson's directorial debut. *Cutlass* tells the story of Lucy (Dakota Fanning) asking for a guitar in a shop window, which sparks her mother to remember when she got her first car, an Olds Cutlass, from her father. This would be Kristen's first project with Dakota Fanning (with whom she would work again in the Twilight Saga and *The Runaways*).

The following year, Kristen filmed *The Yellow Handkerchief*, a drama about three strangers who end up on a road trip through Louisiana, and had a cameo appearance in *Jumper*. She also played Robert De Niro's daughter in *What Just Happened?*, an indie satire about a floundering film producer. The film premiered at the Sundance Film Festival in January 2008. Kristen notes, "Working with Robert De Niro was amazing. He makes

everyone feel important, no matter how small the role."

Up next for Kristen was a part in quirky dark comedy *Adventureland*. Writer/director Greg Mottola was happy that Kristen signed on to play the damaged carnival worker Em, who "needed to be complicated and truly conflicted. We needed an actress who can convey a really believable sense of strength. I knew with Kristen that character wouldn't just be a brat." As with all her characters, in describing Em, Kristen demonstrates a deep empathetic understanding of her: "[She] has no concept of what she really wants out of life. She puts on an act that she's very secure and self-sufficient but she's so not. She realizes too late that she should get over her hang-ups and be good to herself." Kristen praises Greg and his film as well, calling the semi-autobiographical *Adventureland* "very honest; it's not manipulative," and explains, "Greg's films are so real. They're about real people, and it's not trying to be anything. He just takes a snippet of somebody's life." *Adventureland* was released at Sundance in January 2009, and opened to a wide audience on April 3, 2009. The film was generally well-received, though often faulted for not being more like Mottola's earlier comedy *Superbad*.

It was while she was on set in Pittsburgh filming *Adventureland* that Kristen got a visit from *Twilight* director Catherine Hardwicke who wanted her to audition for Bella. Initially, Kristen wasn't interested in the role. Always an advocate of empowered (if damaged) female characters, reading the *Twilight* synopsis led Kristen to conclude that she didn't "want to be a part of something that's presenting this ide-ological idea of what love is to such young girls. I just didn't like that. It was very shallow and vain to me. So she's in love with this guy because he's the hottest thing she's ever seen. That's not what I'm into." But she gave the script a read anyway, and found something more to her taste: "What I got from it was a really, really unhealthy, difficult, impossible love that should be ignored if possible. But it can't be." All of a sudden she was begging for a shot at the role. Auditions often last just a few minutes, but Kristen's was four hours long. Summit knew they had found their Bella. "Her mixture of innocence and longing just knocked me out," said Catherine Hardwicke who was "captivated" by Kristen's Bella.

Kristen, now notoriously, also had a huge influence on the casting of Edward, arguing that Robert Pattinson was the only choice for the role. Once shooting started, Robert and Kristen spent hours analyzing their roles, the books, and what it meant to be a vampire to tease out the internal conflicts and struggles in their characters. The studio tried to get the pair to dial down the intensity, but the stars took their roles seriously. To *Entertainment Weekly*, Kristen ranted, "You knew what you were getting when you hired actors who aren't Disney kids! We're actually going to consider the characters, and not just smile on our marks, and hope we're in focus."

Of Bella, Kristen says, "She acknowledges the fact that she's different and awkward but she owns it and appreciates it. To be self-deprecating while wanting to be in that position is something that I can totally relate to. Not only because she makes a lot of mistakes, but that she's willing to say, 'I made

Best friends Kristen and Nikki Reed have worked together on the Twilight Saga films as well as *K-11*.

these mistakes but I'm not ashamed of them.' I love her honesty."

Their dedication to their roles paid off, earning them the support of the dedicated fan base, and of Stephenie Meyer herself. Commenting on Kristen's embodiment of her beloved protagonist, Stephenie told *USA Today*, "Kristen does a version of Bella that's very strong. And you can see that what she's doing is maturely thought out. In a lot of

> "I didn't want her to be too vulnerable. I didn't want her to be too doe-eyed. That's not necessarily a good thing to promote and I think that helps the movie a lot. You could say about her that she's reckless and shunning things that she should be considering but she's doing them for all the right reasons."
>
> – Kristen on Bella

ways she's a little bit impetuous, but you get the sense that she's very adult about what she's doing. She comes across as a girl who's very serious and who happens to know what she wants."

Twilight went on to gross over $380 million, over nine times its initial filming budget, and added momentum to the already thriving phenomenon boasting fanatic Twihards the world over. In assessing *Twilight*, Kristen is ever modest: "I'm really proud of *Twilight*. I think it's a good movie. It was hard to do, and I think it turned out pretty good. But I don't take much credit for it. So when you show up at these places, and there's literally like a thousand girls and they're all screaming your name, you're like, why? You don't feel like you deserve it." Audiences disagreed, and at the Teen Choice Awards and the MTV Movie Awards the movie cleaned up, with Kristen taking home the prize for Best Female Performance.

After *Twilight*, Kristen told her agent she didn't want to do another big film right away, and appropriately, she landed a part in indie drama *Welcome to the Rileys* opposite James Gandolfini and Melissa Leo, who play a grieving couple who have lost their daughter. Kristen plays Mallory, a stripper and prostitute in Baton Rouge, whom James Gandolfini's character takes under his wing. This gesture, according to Kristen, "shows [Mallory] has the capacity to be a real person and not this shutdown icebox that she's become." To research the role, Kristen spent a few nights actually dancing on a bar at a strip club in New Orleans, learning the moves she'd need in the film.

Kristen revisited Bella in March 2009 when principal photography for *New Moon* began. She was pleased to reprise the role: "I usually only get to fall into character for, like, six weeks. I do little movies and typically they may never see the light of day, so there's this huge grieving process afterwards. Here I get to follow her for an incredibly long time, or at least until the second one. So I'm excited." Since Bella's emotional range is much greater in *New Moon*, it was a more challenging experience for the actress. She explained, "Within a day, I'd have to go back and forth from doing a scene with and without Jacob. So I would have to be dead, zombie Bella who's just absolutely destroyed, to waking up again." Regardless of the challenge, *New Moon* director Chris Weitz felt she handled it just fine. "It's not easy to make falling in love with a vampire look real," he told *USA Today*.

Before *New Moon* would open and eclipse *Twilight*'s box office records, Kristen took the time to film *The Runaways*, a biopic about Joan Jett's teen years, in which Kristen portrayed the celebrated rock star. Having played guitar for eight years already when she took the role, Kristen had the basic skills for the rock 'n' roll performance scenes. But playing a rock icon required a lot of studying, especially when that icon would be on set every day. Before filming, Kristen admitted, "That period with The Runaways was so important. . . . I'm nervous and intimidated. But that's the best way to feel before you do a movie." She threw herself into the task of becoming the rock star, studying tapes Joan had sent to her aunt of her talking and singing at age 14, and asking the star to read specific lines for her or demonstrate certain chords. She had to learn songs like "Cherry Bomb" in only two weeks; she'd be playing the guitar parts herself. Kristen recounted, "I spent every day with Joan. She was a constant for me and has become one of my best friends." Joan was impressed by her doppelganger's performance and her dedication to the role: "I was there to be a resource for Kristen. She watched me a lot — the way I spoke, the way I talked, the way I moved in space, everything. But when it came down to the performing, the most advice I gave her was to trust her instincts. If something was really off then we'd both know it. That occasion really never came." The film also reunited Kristen with Dakota Fanning, who plays Cherie Currie, lead vocalist for The Runaways.

Having wrapped *The Runaways*, it was back to Bella for the filming of *Eclipse* from August to October 2009. Once again, Kristen was returning to a comfortable character, but Bella had changed a lot since the throes of depression she'd experienced in *New Moon*.

Despite her incredible degree of celebrity, her next role was in *K-11*, a small project written and directed by her mother, about a private wing of the L.A. county jail where they put convicts who wouldn't survive among the general population. Kristen and *Twilight* co-star and real-life BFF Nikki Reed play men. With yet another challenging role, it looks like she's determined to live up to Rob's praise when he called her "the best young actress around."

Twilight may have forever altered her career and her profile, but Kristen herself remains pretty much the same person. She's become a little more comfortable in the spotlight, though she still can seem awkward in interviews. The green-eyed beauty continues to insist she's "actually really boring," and go on with her life, spending time with friends and family, reading, and doing some writing. "She's very down-to-earth," says *Into the Wild* co-star Emile Hirsch. "She's not the type of person that will let fame get to her head." Kristen's considered going to college, but admits that structure may not be for her, saying, "I kind of have an authority issue."

But for now Kristen will keep looking for films that speak to her. She confesses, "I can only do a movie if I feel entirely compelled to do it or else in every frame I'm just going to look confused." Undoubtedly there are more troubled but strong women to play in her future, though she's quick to point out it's not her own depression that leads her to play such dark characters. "It's not because I'm a miserable person or sad or whatever," she told the *New York Times.* "The honest, complex roles tend to be serious." In the past she hasn't shied away from difficult roles, and *K-11* indicates that even post-*Twilight* she has no intention of doing so, even if it means taking a risk. "Anything that I do for work, I'm nervous about," says Kristen. "If I'm not nervous about it, then I shouldn't be doing it."

chapter 7

Taylor Lautner as Jacob Black

> **"I've always loved Matt Damon. I love the Bourne series. Brad Pitt, Denzel Washington. But I'd also like to change things up. Not only do I like the action movies, the drama movies that all three of those actors do, I'd also love to challenge myself with different roles. Romantic comedies — I think the best examples would be Gerard Butler, Ryan Reynolds."**
> — Taylor on his acting role models

Discussing the development of Jacob's character, Stephenie Meyer wrote, "Jacob was my first experience with a character taking over — a minor character developing such roundness and *life* that I couldn't keep him locked inside a tiny role. . . . From the very beginning, even when Jacob only appeared in chapter six of *Twilight*, he was so *alive*. I liked him. More than I should for such a small part." Astounding physical transformations aside, Taylor Lautner's greatest contribution to his character Jacob Black is replicating Stephenie's experience for fans — even when placed opposite the older, more experienced, and almost universally adored Robert Pattinson, Taylor has held his own. And while Taylor modestly insists "the fans would love anybody who played Jacob," certainly the teen's down-to-earth, perma-friendly attitude and dazzling white smile had something to do with it. He's charmed audiences, the media, and bolstered the ranks of Team Jacob, leaving audiences howling for more.

Taylor Daniel Lautner was born February 11, 1992, in Grand Rapids, Michigan, to Deborah Lautner, who works for a software company, and Daniel Lautner, a commercial pilot. A younger sister, Makena, followed seven years later. The actor is of French, German, and Dutch descent, though while filming the Twilight Saga he discovered Potawatomi and Ottawa roots on his mother's side.

At age six, Taylor literally kick-started his career when he started taking karate classes at Fabiano's Karate in Holland, Michigan. Already an eager athlete, Taylor was a quick learner, and won three trophies at Nationals after only one year of training. But it would be attending a seminar run by former Blue Power Ranger Mike "Chat" Chaturantabut that would change Taylor's life. Mike Chat had founded Xtreme Martial Arts, a discipline that adds a more gymnastic element to martial arts, with lots of aerial moves and a routine that is choreographed to music. Mike invited Taylor to a six-day camp at UCLA to study the discipline. Taylor gave it a go, and was the youngest student at the camp. "I fell in love," said Taylor. "By the end of the camp, I was doing aerial cartwheels with no hands." The teacher also saw enormous potential in his young new student, potential that stretched beyond martial arts into acting. "He saw that I wasn't shy, that I was confident, that I talked a lot," says the actor. So Mike offered Taylor and his family the opportunity to come live with him in L.A.

for a month, and the marital arts master would try to set up meetings with Hollywood types for his young protégé.

At first, Taylor and his family weren't interested, but after a year of consideration they decided to give it a try. Two days before the end of the month in L.A., Taylor got a call-back for a new Fox TV pilot, *Oliver Beene*. He didn't get the role, but it was enough to convince Taylor and his family that they should keep trying. "I liked it," says Taylor. "Taking on roles that were the opposite of what I could be in real life? That's still my favorite thing." Since they weren't ready to leave Grand Rapids, Taylor started commuting to L.A. for auditions and for marital arts training. "They'd call at 9 or 10 at night, which was 6 or 7 their time, and say, 'We've got an audition tomorrow — can you be here?' We'd leave really early in the morning and get there about noon," recalls Taylor. "I'd go to the audition in the afternoon, take the red-eye back to Grand Rapids, then go to school."

The martial arts training was as intense as the commute, and Taylor dedicated himself to it completely. Mike Chat emphasized to *Rolling Stone* that Taylor earned his success: "People say Taylor got where he is because he has *it*, but he worked hard for it. He practiced like a disciplined Navy SEAL." Taylor is appropriately grateful to the man who shaped him, saying that the intense training "set me up for life. It gave me the confidence, the discipline, and the hard work. Chat used to tell me, 'If you don't give 110 percent, you are not going to get anywhere.'" Taylor went places: he was a four-time World Champion in Xtreme Martial Arts.

Applying the same determination to his fledgling acting career as to his high kicks, he landed his first part, doing voice-over work in a promotion for a *Rugrats* movie. "It was my first job — I was so ecstatic," Taylor remembers. "I thought, 'This is what I've been waiting for.'" As Taylor's career was taking off, his mother's hit a slight obstacle, when her employer, Herman Miller, shut down the Michigan plant where she worked. It was a sign, and the family rallied together for their budding star, relocating to Los Angeles.

Roles started trickling in. Taylor landed a role in the Japanese sci-fi film *Shadow Fury* (2001) about a world where cloning is commonplace. Small television appearances on *The Bernie Mac Show*, *Summerland*, and *My Wife and Kids* followed. He also did some voice work for Frosted Flakes commercials and *What's New, Scooby Doo?*

While he acted, Taylor continued to attend regular school, though his nice-guy attitude couldn't win over kids who were jealous of his success. Taylor confided to *Rolling Stone*, "Because I was acting, when I was in school there was a little bullying going on. Not physical bullying, but people making fun of what I do. . . . I just had to tell myself I can't let this get to me. This is what I love to do. And I'm going to continue doing it." Taylor would continue to attend regular school until the Twilight films made it impossible for him to attend classes, but he completed school by taking the California High School Proficiency Examination.

Then Taylor caught a break, earning a starring role as Sharkboy in the 2005 kids

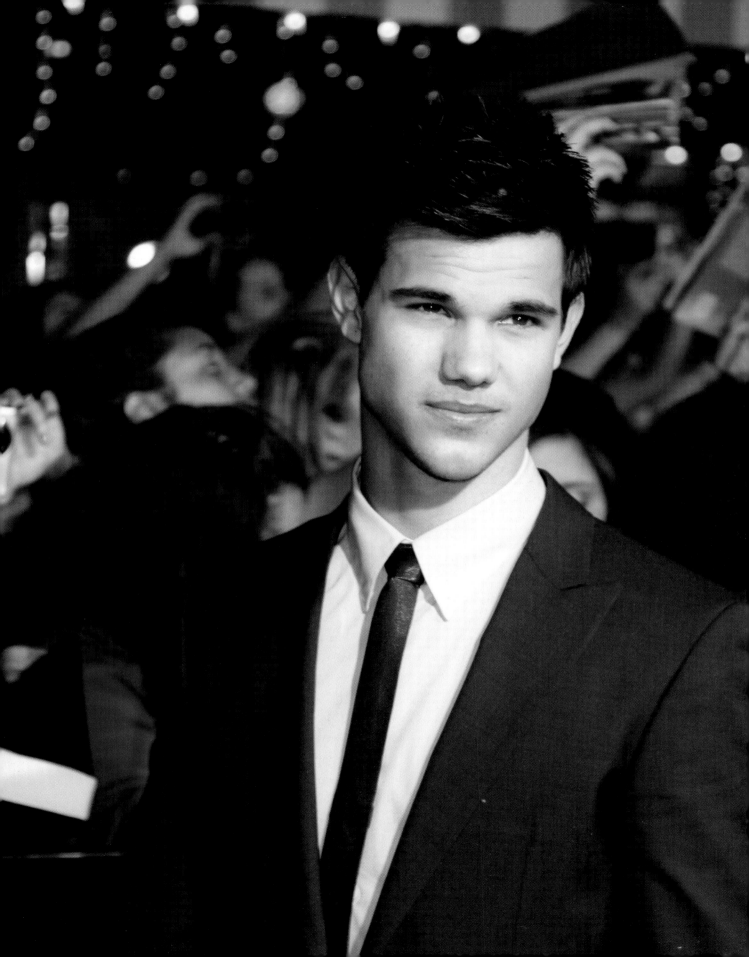

event in the Lautner family, who had put so much faith in Taylor. "My whole family couldn't sleep for, like, a week," recalled the actor. The film is about a lonely boy, Max, who dreams up two superheroes in an alternate universe who take him on an adventure to save the world of his creation. At age 12, Taylor proved he was older than his years, using his extensive martial arts experience to help choreograph his fight scene in the film. Co-star Kristin Davis (best known as Charlotte on *Sex and the City*) recognized his maturity and dedication, and has nothing but praise for the young actor: "He's a great kid and he works really, really, really hard and he had a great professional ethic when I worked with him. [He was] nothing of those negative things that you think of with child actors." Unfortunately the film wasn't the success that Taylor and his family hoped it would be. Nevertheless, it did raise his profile; the actor started being recognized out in public. Taylor recalls, "Ten-year-old boys were the ones who first recognized me. I'd be in the store, and boys would whisper to their moms. Their moms would say, 'Excuse me, are you Sharkboy?'"

Taylor continued to add to his résumé with a role in Steve Martin's *Cheaper by the Dozen 2* (2005), playing not one of the original dozen children, but one of the many children of Eugene Levy's character, Tom, the father of a rival large family. The film wasn't a critical or commercial success, but it did give Taylor the chance to work with established actors like Steve Martin, Bonnie Hunt, and Eugene Levy, as well as young stars like Hilary Duff.

The actor continued landing gigs here and there, including one episode stints on *Love, Inc.*

fantasy-adventure film, *The Adventures of Sharkboy and Lavagirl in 3-D*, from writer/director Robert Rodriguez of *Spy Kids* fame. The director remembers when Taylor came in to audition: "He was the first actor we saw for *Sharkboy and Lavagirl* and we picked him right off. We knew he was the guy. He had so much personality. It's no surprise to me that he was going to go on to great things. He kind of made himself. In fact, he may have walked in fully formed." Landing the role was a huge and *He's a Bully, Charlie Brown*, but after his career had picked up momentum, it temporarily fizzled. Until he got a call about a new project called *Twilight*. At the time, it didn't seem like a big deal. Taylor hadn't read the books and didn't know much about them, but his agent insisted this was major. He went in to meet Catherine Hardwicke and read with Kristen, who thought he was a good choice for the role of Bella's best friend. A month later, Taylor's dad, his agent, and his manager were on the phone, and he could feel it was good news: "I knew. I was sweating, I was so excited."

But the role came with huge expectations, which Jacob discovered as soon as he investigated *Twilight*; he was floored by how popular the series was. He couldn't help but be a little anxious. He explains, "It's hard not to be nervous when you know there's a few million fans out there who are just dying for these movies and you want to make sure it's all top-notch and the best that it can be."

Wanting to be as true to the character as possible, Taylor dug into the books, and was pleased to discover "the series is great. I'm in love with the series. I've never been a book reader, never really read any books besides *Twilight*. Very rarely, maybe an occasional school book." Stephenie Meyer could count one more devotee among her legions of fans. Taylor also took the time to go and speak with some Quileutes in Portland, so he could represent the tribe as faithfully as possible.

For Taylor, slipping into the skin of dependable nice guy Jacob Black was no trouble (aside from an itchy wig). "Jacob is so outgoing, easy to talk to, friendly. So it's fun to play him," says the actor. His co-stars say the same about Taylor. Ashley Greene called him "the total package: sweet, genuine, talented," and Kristen Stewart praises, "He's such a nice human being, he makes you feel morally dysfunctional." Though Taylor didn't have too many scenes in *Twilight*, he and Kristen got to know one another well, so their ease and friendliness would carry over onto the screen. Kristen didn't hesitate to proclaim, "I love that kid. I would do anything for him. I would kill for him, literally."

Taylor's star rose alongside *Twilight*'s; as the film became an international phenomenon, the actor's career finally took off. He took

"That's obviously what you notice first, it's like, 'Pfff,'
a complete physical transformation but if he didn't have
the confidence beforehand to do it then it wouldn't've happened
so fast. He really was the guy; he knew he could do it and that's
the only reason he was able to. . . . He really grew into himself.
He's one of the most steady, good guys I've met."

– Kristen Stewart on
Taylor's *New Moon* transformation

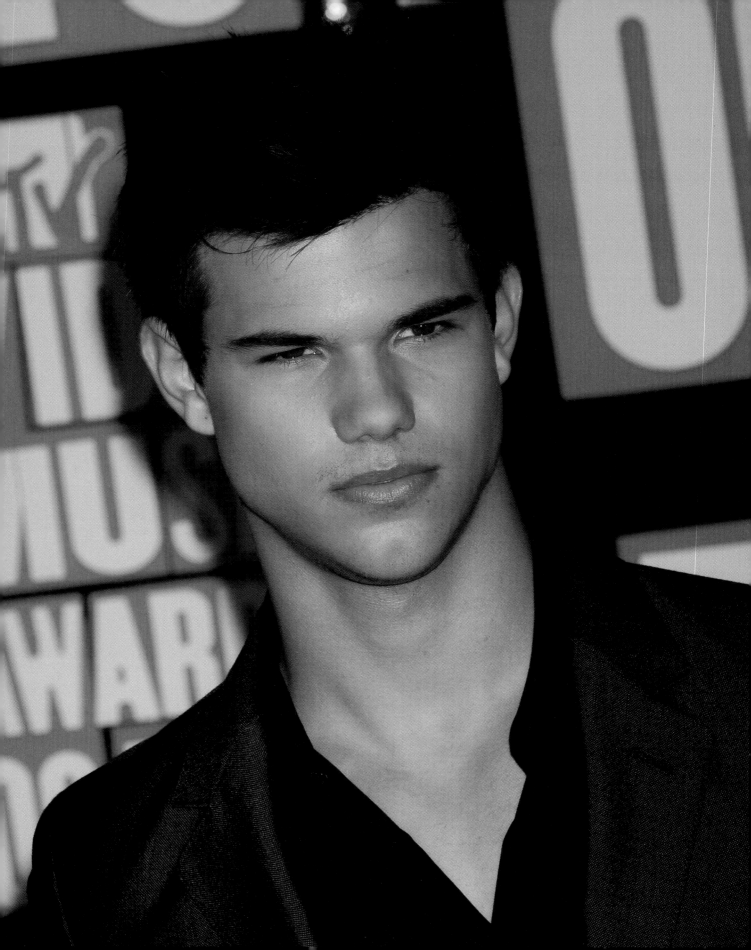

home a Teen Choice Award for Fresh Male Face, was nominated for an MTV Movie Award, and won People's Choice for Favorite Breakout Movie Actor. He'd achieved some success on television as well, landing a starring role as Christian Slater's son on the NBC drama *My Own Worst Enemy*. Slater plays a character with a secret identity: he can be switched from secret agent Edward Albright to middle-class dad Henry Spivey with a chip in his brain. The chip malfunctions in the first episode, so that poor Henry Spivey is often thrust into Edward Albright's dangerous situations. Unfortunately, the show would be canceled before it even finished its first season, leaving storylines dangling after nine episodes on the air.

Nevertheless, working on a show about a man with a split personality would be a good learning experience for Taylor, who could use the experience to play Jacob in *New Moon*. As Summit pushed forward with the sequel, they were unsure if Taylor was the right actor to reprise the role. Jacob undergoes a dramatic physical transformation between the first and the second books, and it was uncertain whether Taylor could make the necessary changes so

quickly. Taylor, drawing on his martial arts training, wasn't about to accept defeat without a fight, and immediately went to work on bulking up. He ignored his nagging fear that he could lose the role, saying, "Honestly, if I would have let myself get to that darkest moment, it wouldn't have been good. So I tried to focus on what I could control the whole time and not let whatever was going on outside get to me. And that's what I did."

The teen wolf blew everyone away when he packed on an astounding 30 pounds of muscle in a mere 11 months. He was at the gym at least six days a week, working out for two to two and a half hours each day. But, says Taylor, "the hardest part was always shoving food down your mouth. I had to be eating every two hours." He needed to consume 3,200 calories over six meals a day. He was always carrying around food, sometimes little bags of meat patties, just to make sure he got enough protein. It paid off. Having gone from a men's size small to a men's large, he convinced the studio that he could phase right along with Jacob.

Director Chris Weitz quickly ascertained that it wasn't just his new bulging biceps that

"I love Jacob and Bella's relationship. It's very different from Edward and Bella's. Jacob and Bella start off as really good friends. They become best friends — they can tell each other anything, they do whatever together, ride motorcycles. I love that. And then their relationship starts growing into more and more, and you wonder if they're going to go past friends. I love being able to do that."

– Taylor on his favorite part of playing Jacob

made Taylor right for the role, and he was eager to tell the media: "I think that Taylor is really going to surprise people in the movie. People have seen his body and all that stuff and it's a shocker because it's hard to believe that anyone can be quite so carved. But he actually delivers a really great performance. He wasn't just exercising all day, he was also reading the book quite a lot."

With the open window between *New Moon* and *Eclipse*, Taylor was able to branch out and land a role in the Garry Marshall ensemble romantic comedy *Valentine's Day* (2010), which focuses on the intertwined stories of several characters on the day of romance. It's possible cupid struck while he was on set, with rumors pairing the actor with another Taylor, superstar country singer Taylor Swift. Though neither officially confirmed the pairing, the two played coy with the media, alluding to one another in their *SNL* monologues.

When *Eclipse* was in the can, it was back to normal life. Taylor still lives with his family in L.A., and has signed up for some online courses at a community college. And while the media would love another story of a teen star gone wild, Taylor couldn't be more responsible. He outlined his average day to *Rolling Stone*: "When I'm at home I wake up, I go to the gym, I get in my car, I drive down to L.A., and I go to meetings all day. Then I come back, eat dinner, see my family, see friends, go to bed, and then do the same thing all over again the next day." Part of the reason he's still on the straight and narrow is the influence of his family. Explained his father, Dan, "Because of all that's happening for him, we want him to do normal things. We kept him in public school as long as we could, so he could be with his peers. We give him responsibilities at home — chores he has to do. He gets an allotted allowance and he has to budget it. We're trying to teach him things, so that when he goes out on his own, he'll be prepared." And although Taylor may be all over movie posters and magazine covers, his parents also try to keep his priorities in line. "It's key as parents to talk to him about what's important in life, because it's not being a movie star," says Dan. "We tell Taylor, 'You've been given this opportunity. Be thankful for it, because it may disappear one day.'"

If you ask Taylor's co-stars, his parents have gotten the message across. Fellow wolf-pack member Chaske Spencer noted, "His parents raised him really well. He's a 'please and thank you' kind of guy; just an all-around sweetheart. He is a good human being and I am very impressed with how he conducts himself in terms of everything [happening] around him. He is very down-to-earth and very levelheaded."

With his head on his shoulders and his good heart, Taylor will just keep acting, training, and playing sports. As for future roles? "I love action films. I'd love to do an action drama. I'm always looking to give my character something action-oriented to do," Taylor told *Interview*. In the meantime, he's enjoying the ride, just like Jacob would, and trying to keep it real, since he knows an opportunity like this only comes along once in a blue moon.

The Cullens

chapter 8

ASHLEY GREENE
AS ALICE CULLEN

❋ ❋ ❋

When Ashley Michele Greene started her Hollywood career, it involved spending some serious time in front of cameras — but it was for fashion photographers' rather than movie cameras. Ashley left Wolfson High School in Jacksonville, Florida, midway through her senior year (she already had enough credits to graduate) to move to L.A. and become an actress, but had more luck modeling at first.

Until her decision to leave, Ashley had been nothing but a model student. She took honors classes and was heavily involved in extra-curricular activities: she won awards for tae kwon do, she took acting and dance classes, and at University Christian School (which she attended until tenth grade), she was part of an all-star cheerleading squad.

Born February 21, 1987, she was only 17 when she decided to strike out on her own, but her parents, Joe Greene, owner of a concrete company, and Michele Greene, who works at an insurance company, decided to give her their full support. "It was scary," says Ashley's mother. "There were a lot of late nights where we lay in bed and talked about it. But it's kind of a Catch-22: if you raise your kid to follow their dreams, you're kind of on the hook."

Her mom helped her move to L.A. and get set up in a new apartment; while Joe and Michele were nervous, they had nothing but faith in their daughter. Her father remembers, "I think we all had confidence that she had all the skills and attitude to be one of the people who actually makes it out there, that it's some-

thing she'd fall into. She's always been a social butterfly — even though she's pretty, she's still real nice."

But despite her parents' confidence, Ashley was forced to face some hard truths early on. Acting work was scarce for someone with no experience, and at 5'5" she wasn't tall enough to be a runway model, so she was nudged toward commercial work instead. What first appeared to be a setback actually was a step forward, since her early difficulty led her to acting classes and inspiration in the form of a dedicated teacher. Ashley relates, "The teacher who I was taught by was just so passionate about it. He was amazing! I fell in love with it, instantly. I was like, 'This is so what I want to do! I don't want to model.'"

Ashley started auditioning for TV roles but, as with most aspiring actors, steady work was hard to come by. She'd go to five auditions a week and be lucky to come home with one small part a month. Some of her early jobs included guest spots on MTV's *Punk'd*, *MADtv*, and the crime drama *Crossing Jordan*. She had a bit more luck with *Desire*, landing seven episodes on the short-lived telenovela about two restaurateurs on the run from the New Jersey mafia.

After that part things slowed down, and Ashley's only screen credit for 2007 was as a McDonald's customer in *Kings of California* starring Michael Douglas and Evan Rachel Wood. It may have been a small-fry part but it was Ashley's film debut.

It was a hard time for the actress; she admitted to *Nylon*, "I went through a stage where — well, you know, I was 20 and drinking and whatnot. But I deal with things better now. I refuse to cry over [failing auditions] because it's just not worth it. But I am extremely passionate about acting, so in many ways they were all a learning process for me."

There were a couple more small roles, one appearance in the legal drama *Shark* and a part as Kim #4 (it's never good when there's a number beside your character's name) in the straight-to-DVD horror-comedy *Otis*. But Ashley was about to move on to a character much more beloved than Kim #1, 2, or 3: her breakthrough role as psychic vampire sis Alice Cullen in *Twilight*.

Her management stressed that this audition was a really big deal. They told the actress, "You're going into this casting office and they're really tough, but they're really good. Don't mess up. This is a book series. It should be good. If it does well, you could do a couple films." She remembers, "I really didn't know what a big deal it was, but I knew it was something." Since she wasn't provided with much to work with for the audition, Ashley went out and devoured Stephenie Meyer's first book in a day and a half, and calls it "brilliant and un-putdown-able."

The audition process lasted four months, but it was worth the wait: "I came in probably, like, five times before I actually got the role — and then I went home for Christmas and literally just had to wait and wait. I thought that I didn't get it again, and then I got the call that I was Alice and I freaked out and called my dad and mom."

Ashley originally auditioned for Bella's role, but the casting directors wisely had her audition for Alice instead. It was a decision that greatly pleased Stephenie Meyer, who was

shocked at how closely Ashley matched her own vision of Alice. "On first look, the one that really jumped out was Ashley Greene as Alice," said Meyer. "I saw a picture of her and just thought, 'You found Alice! Oh, my gosh!'"

Ashley also felt that the role was a perfect fit. Though her psychic abilities leave something to be desired, the actress could relate to her character in other ways: "I can definitely understand the intensity behind protecting her family." And what about Alice's passion for fashion? "Of course, I get the shopping. Every girl loves shopping." Deep down, Ashley knew that she was made for this role. "It was one of those monumental things in your life," she relates. "There are some parts where you're just like, 'This is my part, and nobody can do a better job,' and that was this."

After *Twilight* stormed the box office and was embraced by dedicated fans all over the globe, Ashley's life, both personal and professional, changed dramatically. She told *Vanity Fair*: "With the success of the film, there are a lot of things you get offered, places people want you to go just to have you there, and I really haven't been able to do that. Between this and other films, I've just been working. You know, I was a struggling actor, and I was modeling to pay bills. I was worried about rent, and I was living with two other people. To go from that to me going, 'I need a break, I need a day off' is a crazy thing. It's good, and it's tiring, but my mom being able to see what I'm doing every single day on the internet? It's crazy! From nobody really knowing or really caring who you are or what you do to suddenly making headlines with what you're eating, where you're going, who you're hanging out

and having coffee with is nuts. But I guess it helps when I'm walking into these rooms with directors and producers, all of a sudden they know who I am."

Bolstered by a 2009 Teen Choice Award for Fresh Face Female, she was kept busy with more projects than even Alice Cullen could have foreseen. Beyond filming *New Moon* and *Eclipse*, she played Summer in the Canadian thriller *Summer's Moon* about hitchhiking gone terribly wrong. The film went straight to DVD, but it's a huge improvement over Ashley's pre-*Twilight* direct-to-DVD project — she's gone from Kim #4 to the titular role.

Ashley also landed the role of Rhonda in *Radio Free Albemuth*, a sci-fi adaptation of the 1985 Philip K. Dick novel. The film stars Canadian singer-songwriter Alanis Morissette in the lead role.

Ashley was slated to reunite with *Twilight* co-star and friend Kellan Lutz in the indie flick *Strife*, which followed three friends as they battled through the gritty day-to-day realities of gangs and drugs on the streets of L.A., but that movie "never came through" and both actors moved on. Luckily, they found themselves once again working together, this time in *Warrior*, a movie about lacrosse that has the erstwhile "siblings" now playing lovers. Ashley is just pleased to have the chance to work with Lutz once again: "There's something cool where me and Kellan get the opportunity to work together a lot. I love him to death."

As if those projects weren't enough, Ashley worked on another indie film, *Skateland*, starring Shiloh Fernandez, an actor Catherine Hardwicke revealed was one of the top four contenders for the Edward Cullen role. *Skateland* is a light-hearted coming-of-age story set in 1983, which gives Ashley a chance to trade in her Alice Cullen pixie cut for some serious Farrah Fawcett hair.

With her career taking off, Ashley's future aspirations involve playing strong female parts like her acting role model Charlize Theron, and broadening her already considerable range: "I want to stay away from the typical high school characters, like the hot girl and the mean girl. That's boring. You don't get to transform. I don't want to stick to one genre or one role. I just want to take part in a bunch of different roles and become a bunch of different characters. I definitely want to do an action film and be a superhero, I want to play a villain, I want to do a period piece, and I want to do a love story. We'll see what order they come in. I want to do a little bit of everything." While she's come a long way from Wolfson High, it's clear that one thing hasn't changed — she's got big dreams and she's willing to risk it all chasing them.

JACKSON RATHBONE
AS JASPER HALE

❋ ❋ ❋

He may be greeted by screaming fans when he goes out to dinner with his family, but Jackson Rathbone's father insists fame hasn't changed his son. "He sees himself as just Jackson Rathbone, and so many people see him as bigger than life, he's just a good kid that's done well."

Monroe Jackson Rathbone V was born December 21, 1984, in Singapore to parents Randee and Monroe Jackson Rathbone IV. His father worked for Mobil Oil, so the family traveled all over the world to Indonesia, London, Connecticut, California, and Norway, before settling in Texas.

Jackson started acting in the sixth grade, when he became involved with The Pickwick Players, a community theater group in his hometown of Midland, Texas. The troupe put on shows around four times a year. It was a romance from the start. "When I started being on stage, I fell in love with it," says the actor.

It's no surprise to fans of his band, 100 Monkeys, that Jackson's earliest theatrical experience was with musicals. Later, he became absorbed in Shakespeare, though in both cases, he was always the character actor rather than the leading man. This was just fine by Jackson, who stated, "I've never found [leading roles] as interesting as the supporting characters and the side parts, who drive the story a little bit more. I've always loved the character of Iago from *Othello*, and Benedick from *Much Ado About Nothing*, and Judas from *Jesus Christ Superstar*. I find the characters that have these dark sides, or even extremely light sides, more interesting. I try to find extremes."

To improve his acting skills, Jackson enrolled in the Interlochen Arts Academy in Michigan for his junior and senior year of high school. There he majored in acting, but also developed his interest in music. At Interlochen he roomed with 100 Monkeys co-founder, actor Ben Graupner, and also befriended future Monkeys drummer Ben Johnson.

Upon graduation, Jackson took off for L.A. to pursue his dream of acting. His first success was in commercials and as an interviewer for

Disney 411, followed by a guest spot on the crime drama *Close to Home*. The following year, Jackson made his debut on the big screen in the 2006 thriller *Pray for Morning*, about six students who break into a hotel where five high schoolers had been murdered 20 years earlier.

Jackson also shot two episodes of *The O.C.*, one of which also featured his future *Twilight* co-star Nikki Reed ("Heavy Lifting"). After many bit parts and one-offs, Jackson's perseverance would finally pay off with a recurring role as rich heartthrob Nicholas Fiske on the ABC Family drama *Beautiful People*. Regrettably, the show was canceled after 16 episodes. After parts in TV movies *Valley of Light* and *The War at Home*, Jackson went back to the big screen playing a hippie in the Rob Schneider comedy *Big Stan*.

When Jackson heard about *Twilight*, he took a pretty casual approach to the whole affair, not knowing the part of Jasper Hale could propel him into the pop culture stratosphere. "I auditioned two or three months before filming started, and I just walked to the audition, because the studio was close to my house, so I'd walk there with my guitar and I played it in the waiting room," he explained.

But when Jackson's large extended family all started calling him to tell him how excited they were that he'd be in *Twilight*, the actor realized he was a part of something big. (Though nothing could have prepared him for the overwhelming fan response. "I feel like a Jonas Brother!" he said of the screaming crowds at TwiCon.)

When it came to relating to his bloodsucking alter-ego, what tied them together was a Southern upbringing, regardless of the century it took place in. "I just tried to keep up the values that I believed Jasper was instilled with, when he was a kid, and I think those were fairly similar to the ones I grew up with," says Jackson. "I just tried to play the more humanistic element of him, while at the same time masking that monster element, which is what he's trying to do anyway."

When *Twilight* took off and the scripts started rolling in, Jackson knew that he had the fans to thank for his flourishing career. He told MTV, "*Twilight* has given me, and a lot of the other actors on *Twilight*, a much wider fan base, and they've been so supportive of us, and that's really what we need. As an actor, you need an audience to practice your craft. A painter can paint alone, a photographer can take pictures alone, a musician can play — but as an actor, you need someone to watch you, and we couldn't have a better audience. . . . I've been able to do a lot more films because of them."

With *Twilight* in his pocket, Jackson lined up several other films. He starred in the *Donnie Darko* sequel, *S. Darko*, which picks up the story of Donnie's little sister and has just as many mind-bending hallucinations as the original. He can also be seen on the big screen starring in *Hurt*, a gothic thriller.

Jackson started work on his first leading role in the 2009 horror film *Dread*. Jackson plays Stephen Grace, who is part of a group doing an academic study of fear, which eventually morphs into a *Saw*-esque experiment forcing study participants to live through their worst fears. Despite his professed fondness for supporting roles, Jackson certainly doesn't dread his new position. "This is a character that has a lot of development, a lot of progression,"

he told MTV. "I like roles that I can sink my teeth into." Plus, he admits, "When you're off camera, it's fun to chase someone around covered in blood."

Jackson's other buzzworthy project is *The Last Airbender*, a fantasy film written by M. Night Shyamalan of *Sixth Sense* fame. The film is a live action adaptation of the animated series *Avatar: The Last Airbender*, in which a group of young warriors try to save the world with their martial arts skills and ability to manipulate the elements. Jackson was excited to work with Shyamalan, and calls the project "an action-packed, epic film," and noted, "It's

a chance to do something a little funnier. Something less serious than Jasper." He'll also appear in *The Girlfriend*, a film about a man with Down's syndrome who falls for a small-town single mom.

When he's not filming back-to-back movies, Jackson dedicates his time to his band, 100 Monkeys. The name comes from a story about monkeys learning to wash sweet potatoes and the critical mass required — 100 monkeys — for the idea to spread across a region's population. Jackson explains, "It's basically the idea of the collective consciousness. As soon as so many people have one idea or one belief, it affects the greater majority." It's also a great excuse to take pictures of the band members in giant banana costumes.

The band originally started with Jackson and his roommate Ben Graupner, but has now expanded to include Ben Johnson, Jerad Anderson, and M. Lawrence Abrams. 100 Monkeys has adopted a jam band style of improvisational playing, their music "ranging from an old-school rock 'n' roll blues mentality to a funky kind of music." The band released two CDs in 2009, *Monster De Lux* and *Creative Control*, and are quickly following it up with a third album, *Grape*. Their music is all available on iTunes and at 100monkeysmusic.com.

To the delight of their fans, the band announced a 100-city tour in late 2009. A highlight of their live performances? The band members are all accomplished musicians and like to pull "monkey switcharoos" during the set, where everyone switches instruments. Jackson himself can play guitar, keyboards, and bass, as well as some mandolin and banjo. Despite the band's expanding fan base, Jackson isn't about to abandon acting to become a rock star. He stated, "I'm an actor, first and foremost, but the music, for me, is my soul."

As for the rest of his career, like many actors, Jackson has hopes of directing one day. But since he didn't go to school for filmmaking, he's learning whatever he can on set. "I try to study as much as I can from the producers, the cinematographers, the directors, and the writers," said the actor. "I ask as many questions as I can, to pick as many brains as I can, just to figure out what moves people." He's also started a fledgling production company to promote the talented people he knows, and has written two pilots for TV shows.

Whether it's international recognition as an actor or sold-out gigs as a musician, Jackson's pretty satisfied with how things have gone so far: "I've been setting off, since I was 18, on the path I wanted to take, and I think I'm on it now."

NIKKI REED
AS ROSALIE HALE

❀ ❀ ❀

Although people often think that the Hollywood limelight can be a negative influence on young people, for Nikki Reed, making a film is what helped bring her life back under control.

Nicole Houston Reed was born May 17, 1988, in west Los Angeles, California, the second child of Cheryl Houston, a hair stylist, and Seth Reed, an art director (you can see his work in movies such as *Minority Report*, *Fight Club*, and *Miami Vice*). Her parents divorced when she was two, and she lived with her mother, although her father continued to parent her. In fact, one of his father's girlfriends, then–production designer Catherine Hardwicke, would have an important and lasting influence on Nikki's life.

Hardwicke describes the young Nikki as "such a fun, crazy, like awesome, lively kid — really creative." But before she'd even reached her teen years, Nikki started to skid off track. She started "hanging out with the bad girls, ditching school, smoking weed, and messing around with boys." In short, "I grew up fast," says the actress.

This was when Hardwicke stepped in. She tried anything to get Nikki invested in something that wasn't self-destructive. After trying things like surfing and Jane Austen novels, Hardwicke suggested writing a screenplay together. The first draft of *Thirteen* was the result of a six-day collaboration between the two women. "I knew nothing about writing," Nikki told *Entertainment Weekly*. "But Catherine wasn't 13 and I was, so that's where the movie got its basic outline. It's my voice."

Released in 2003, *Thirteen* unflinchingly exposes the pressures and temptations of being a young teenage girl when straight-as-an-arrow Tracy (Evan Rachel Wood) is befriended by bad girl Evie (Nikki Reed), who leads her into a world of petty crime, drinking, drugs, and sexual experimentation. Holly Hunter plays Tracy's beleaguered yet distracted mother, and received an Academy Award nomination for the poignant role. The film was a hit at the Sundance Film Festival, winning the Director's Award, and Evan Rachel Wood and Nikki Reed were also both honored with Golden Globe nominations for their performances.

Despite Nikki's stellar performance, she had never intended to act in the movie, but they couldn't find a young actress who was comfortable reading Evie's lines, let alone embodying the reckless role. The actress remembers, "Acting was not what I wanted to do. I was a shy kid, didn't go to drama camp or take acting lessons. I shied away from all that. I was a real bookworm."

The film's inflammatory honesty gave Nikki instant notoriety; she was widely portrayed as a "bad girl" at 14. Nikki took the money she earned from *Thirteen* and emancipated herself from her parents, moving out into her own apartment. She tried to go back to school, but found that "it was really horrible writing a film about not being able to fit in and hoping this would help and then going back and having the problem start all over again." So Nikki dropped out of high school and turned to home schooling.

Nikki found other roles in independent films coming her way. She played Zane, a young prostitute who seduces a rabbi in 2005's *Man of God*, a low-budget black-and-white film, which Nikki calls "very cool and very artsy" and asserts she was "very proud to be a part of it."

Nikki followed *Man of God* with Catherine Hardwicke's second directorial project, 2005's *Lords of Dogtown*, a film about the development of professional skateboarding in 1970s Venice Beach. Here Nikki would work alongside soon-to-be best friend (and longtime boyfriend of Kristen Stewart) Michael Angarano. Around the same time, Nikki would also get to act alongside heavyweights such as Forest Whitaker and Marcia Gay Harden in *American Gun*.

Many actors must work their way through modeling, commercial work, or small television roles before they get parts like the ones Nikki started out with, but the actress's unconventional career brought her to television years after having established herself as an indie-film success. In 2006, she did a six-episode stint on *The O.C.*, playing Sadie, a love interest for Ryan Atwood (Benjamin McKenzie). Though she was initially reluctant to take the role on the hit drama about the angsty woes

> "The punch line for Rosalie is that she's the most beautiful person in the world. I'm very aware that *that* is Rosalie and *this* is me, and that beauty is subjective. I don't think anyone can fill those shoes."
>
> — Nikki Reed

of the rich and beautiful, Nikki's management team talked her into it. The role added diversity to Nikki's portfolio, and she commented, "I'm doing what I love by doing independent films and writing constantly, but I'm also doing television that's very PG and so I'm doing both ends." *The O.C.*'s creator Josh Schwartz was glad to have Nikki on board, calling her "a great naturalistic actress." Nikki also continued her foray into TV that year with a guest spot on the legal drama *Justice*.

Even with lighter television roles, Nikki demonstrated she hadn't forgot her indie roots with her role in *Mini's First Time*. She plays another young prostitute, this time one who seduces her stepfather (Alec Baldwin) and convinces him to help her kill her alcoholic mother. She wasn't even old enough to be shown naked on camera for the racy role, but director Nick Guthe called the actress "an old soul . . . a 30-year-old in a 16-year-old girl's body."

In 2007's *Cherrytown*, Reed's character is once again involved with an older man, this time using him to get into a prestigious music school, and willing to use nude photos as blackmail. The same year, Reed also appeared in the pilot for the supernatural TV series *Reaper*; her unaired scenes can be found on YouTube.

By early 2008, Nikki had been cast in her third Catherine Hardwicke film (though Nikki stresses there was no intervention on the director's part), this time as "the most beautiful woman in the world," resentful vampire Rosalie Hale. It was a role that required a major physical transformation for the dark-haired, olive-skinned beauty, and Nikki was subjected to skin bleaching and up to 36 hours in a stylist's chair to achieve Rosalie's blonde locks.

Although Rosalie's character isn't fully explored until *Eclipse*, Nikki worked hard to add as much dimension to the icy Cullen as possible. Having spent her share of time in the spotlight, Nikki identifies with Rosalie's desire to live a normal life. "Rosalie really just wanted to be normal; that's what she's always wanted," Nikki told MTV. "She just wanted to be like an average young woman who got married and had a family."

Unlike many of her fellow cast mates, Nikki had already had her share of celebrity, so while she benefited from the unforeseen success of *Twilight*, she'd already had her breakthrough role at the tender age of 14. Nikki balanced making *Twilight* films with several other projects including a starring role in the 2008 film *Familiar Strangers* about family relationships at Thanksgiving, 2009's *Chain Letter*, a thriller about the deadly consequences of not forwarding chain mail, and *Last Day of Summer*, about a disgruntled fast-food employee who kidnaps a pretty girl (Nikki) on the last day of his summer job. Nikki also grabbed a starring role in the film *Privileged*.

Nikki transitioned from playing the singularly stunning Rosalie to playing a man in

K-11 along with her close pal Kristen Stewart. Nikki looked forward to this dramatic transformation. "It is going to be very challenging. I am not going to run away from it, but it certainly takes a lot of preparation mentally and physically," she explained.

Despite being an in-demand actress, Nikki doesn't plan to be seen on the screen for the rest of her career. She wants to continue her work as a producer (she got her first credit on *Last Day of Summer*), to direct, and to continue writing. She's written several other screenplays and has been offered numerous writing deals, but has passed them up because, the self-assured actress says, "I know what my voice is." She's also working on a novel, and remarked, "It's unbelievable. I can write forever." In any case, the multi-talented Nikki is keeping her options open and will continue to play by her own rules, having long ago learned that "nothing is worth anything if you're not happy with what you're doing."

KELLAN LUTZ
AS EMMETT CULLEN

❋ ❋ ❋

Although now Kellan Lutz can't go to local high school football games without being recognized, being an actor, let alone a successful one, was something he never would have dreamed of as a kid with a humble Midwest upbringing. "I never knew you could be an actor," Lutz told *Nylon*. "It was magic-castle stuff."

Born March 15, 1985, in Dickinson, North Dakota, Kellan Christopher Lutz is a middle child with one sister and six brothers. His parents divorced when he was six, and times were often tough for the Lutz family: "I've lived out of a van, a lot of times in my life. After the divorce, I had it really hard and we were scraping pennies. I didn't live out of a box or anything, but poverty was around." His family moved around the Midwest before finally settling in Arizona, where his mother remarried.

Kellan's introduction to acting came through his church, where he performed in Christmas plays and the production of *Oliver Twist*. His first paying job wasn't as an actor but as a model, which he got into in his early teens. Despite some modeling success in Arizona, it didn't seem like a plausible career to Kellan, and he enrolled at Chapman University in Orange County, California, to study chemical engineering. But Kellan quickly realized his heart wasn't in it. He admits, "I wanted to go to a good school to make mom happy, but it became too much pressure. I was trying to live the life that she wanted me to." He started going to acting classes and auditions. When it came down to writing finals or going to an audition, acting won out. Kellan concedes, "[Being a chemical engineer] was a respectable job. But my personality needs more. The rush of having an audition or becoming another character was awesome."

When he moved to L.A., he recalls, "I saw the passion in everyone's eyes, and just really fell for it and loved it and wanted it. I saw how much fun people were having, enjoying life. In a way, it keeps you young." Kellan continued modeling (in campaigns for Abercrombie & Fitch, Levi's, and in Hilary Duff's "With Love" perfume campaign and music video), and the acting roles started trickling in. At age 20, he appeared in single episodes of *The Bold and the Beautiful*, *CSI: NY*, and *Six Feet Under*.

He landed two episodes of *Summerland* and eight episodes of *The Comeback*, an HBO series starring Lisa Kudrow.

In 2006, Kellan made his first film appearance in the comedy/drama *Stick It* about a rebellious teen forced to go to an elite gymnastics academy. Later that same year, the actor could be spotted on the big screen again in *Accepted*, a comedy about college rejects who start their own university. He continued to do some minor television work with guest roles on *CSI* and *Heroes*.

His first major project was in the HBO miniseries *Generation Kill*, a TV adaptation from the book by Evan Wright that relates his time as a reporter embedded in a military unit during the Iraq War, focusing on the 2003 1st Reconnaissance Marines. The actors prepared with a two-week boot camp; filmed in South Africa, Mozambique, and Namibia; worked with live equipment; and endured an exhausting shooting schedule, filming six days a week for seven months. Kellan loved it, developing a bond with fellow cast members: "It was tough but being with 39 other guys, it was a family."

It was while he was in Africa that Kellan heard about *Twilight*. Reading the script, "it felt so new and fresh, not the typical 'let's kill the vampire with a pitchfork' idea. It was really unique." His management team put him forward for the Edward role, but being tied up with *Generation Kill*, Kellan was unable to fly back to audition and knew a taped audition was unlikely to make it back to America. The opportunity passed. After he returned home to Los Angeles, Kellan got word that the original Emmett had fallen through. His agent got him an audition the next day, and after passing the first round, Kellan was flown out to Oregon the day after to audition for Catherine Hardwicke. She saw Emmett's loveable charm in the affable actor, and Kellan started work a few days later.

Thrown into the film at the last minute, Kellan had no idea of the scope of the *Twilight* phenomenon. He hadn't read the books, but when pal Ashley Greene leant them to him, he quickly plowed through the first three. (*Breaking Dawn* had not yet been published.) He felt he was a perfect fit for the character, who he describes as "the tough guy, the protector, but he's a big old teddy bear to his little brother. He's a goofball, but when he snaps, he's menacing and there's no stopping him." The most important thing Kellan takes from the role is Emmett's general joie-de-vivre. "I mean he is how I live my life. I live such a, or I try to live such a carefree, stress-free life and I'm just so happy to wake up and be alive and just have a good night's sleep," says Kellan. "I'm so thankful for my life and everyone around it and my family. And, you know, just life is good and we should always live life as happy as we can."

Twilight catapulted Kellan into the spotlight, and he found more work coming his way. He joined the cast of the new *90210* as George Evans, "the cocky dick of the school," who appeared in six episodes of season 1. After acting in this quintessential teen soap, Kellan did a 180 and shot a couple episodes of *Valley Peaks*, which spoofs teen dramas just like *90210*.

Kellan is now bombarded with movie scripts, so many that he admits, "I feel like

that's all I'm doing is reading scripts." Aside from *New Moon* and *Eclipse*, his other post-*Twilight* film projects include a starring role in *Warrior* (with Ashley Greene), in which he plays a lacrosse star who has recently lost his father, and high-school jock Dean in the 2010 remake of *A Nightmare on Elm Street*.

Though Kellan's physique makes him a shoe-in for jock-type roles, the actor is looking for something that's more of a challenge. His ideal role? A tortured drug-addict. "I'd love to be able to show some depth and to cry and to show life's troubles," says the star. "I love the edgier stuff and the independent stuff."

When he has free time, Kellan has proven himself a dedicated volunteer. He's been offering up his time since he lived in Arizona, supporting charities such as the Boys and Girls Club, the Humane Society, and Royal Family Kids Camp, which gives a regular camp experience to abused children. It's no surprise that the self-confessed "goofball" star loves kids ("I can't wait to have a couple Kellans running around"), and finds his volunteer experience extremely rewarding: "It was great, just being able to reach out to these kids and give them an adult figure, or an elder, who they can actually look up to, and have someone show them love and help them feel love."

For the time being, Kellan is enjoying his success. He admits he loves red carpets and Hollywood life, though he hasn't let it go to his

head. He says of his co-star and real-life pal Ashley Greene, "We're normal people. It's not going to change us. I'm happy to be a part of it and wherever it takes us, it's only for the best."

PETER FACINELLI AS CARLISLE CULLEN

❅ ❅ ❅

Long before he played a vampire patriarch with a conscience, Peter Facinelli was inspired to act by two other loveable bad boys — Butch Cassidy and the Sundance Kid. When he was in third grade he read a picture book biography of Robert Redford, and when he watched the 1969 classic movie, he was captivated. "I loved what Robert Redford and Paul Newman did, and I thought, 'That's what I want to do,'" Peter told *People*.

It was a big dream for someone of humble origins. Born November 26, 1973, in Queens, New York, the actor-to-be was the son of Italian immigrants Pierino, a waiter, and Bruna, a homemaker, and little brother to JoAnne, Lisa, and Linda. Peter has fond memories of the Ozone Park neighborhood he grew up in: "It was a real community. All the neighbors knew each other and watched out for one another."

When he told his parents he wanted to be an actor, they didn't believe it since their son was so shy. Peter remembers, "My family kind of laughed it off because they didn't think it was possible." The aspiring actor let his dream rest for a while, deciding to pursue a career in law instead. He enrolled in pre-law at St. John's University, seeking the excitement of courtroom drama, but quickly realized that lawyers actually want to stay *out* of court. Peter hadn't forgotten his dream; he decided to transfer to New York University to study acting. He broke it to his parents gently: "I told my parents, 'I'm going to transfer to NYU because as a lawyer you need theatrical skills to win over the jury.'"

When it came time to tell his parents that he'd be winning over audiences instead of juries, Peter was sure to share his first success with his parents. "I remember bringing my paycheck to my dad," says the actor. "It was $150. I never went back [to NYU]. I'm 15 credits shy." That paycheck was for his part in *Angela*, a 1995 film in which the young actor played the devil. Perhaps it was a good omen for Peter's career that the film won awards at Sundance, the annual festival started by the very actor who inspired Peter in the first place.

After *Angela*, the actor switched to the small screen for a while, appearing in a string of TV movies: *The Runaways* (1995), *The Price of Love* (1995), *An Unfinished Affair* (1996), *After Jimmy* (1996), and *Calm at Sunset* (1996). Though Facinelli had lead roles in *After Jimmy* and *Calm at Sunset*, it was *An Unfinished Affair* that would have the biggest impact on his life. On set he fell for actress Jennie Garth. They married January 20, 2001.

Peter returned to the big screen with supporting roles in *Foxfire* (1996), *Touch Me* (1997), *Welcome to Hollywood* (1998) and lead roles in *Telling You* (1998) and *Dancer, Texas Pop. 81* (1998), though he would really gain some pop culture currency with the 1998 teen comedy *Can't Hardly Wait*. Auditioning for the role of insensitive jock Mike Dexter, Peter decided to go straight to the heart of the role:

he walked into the room and started doing push-ups. It got him the part, for which he's still remembered. Peter explained the continued relevance of the film to MTV: "I think people just identify with the movie. I remember in high school there were the cliques. Every table at lunch had a different group. . . . I still get people that are going through high school now, and they're like, 'I love *Can't Hardly Wait*!' And I'm like, 'You were five when that movie came out!'"

From there Peter's big screen roles kept piling up: he starred alongside Danny Devito and Kevin Spacey in 1999's *The Big Kahuna*, and with pop group All Saints in the widely panned *Honest* (2000); he did sci-fi in *Supernova* and rom-com in *Ropewalk* (both 2000); he appeared in box office successes *Riding in Cars with Boys* (2001) and *The Scorpion King* (2002).

In 2002, Peter made his return to the small screen, starring in the Fox action/drama *Fastlane*. A *Miami Vice*–esque exploration of L.A.'s criminal underworld, the series followed two undercover LAPD cops (Peter and Bill Bellamy). Peter called the cinematic series "pure entertainment"; the show was popular but extremely expensive to make, and it was canceled after one season.

The actor had better success with a recurring role on the firmly established HBO cult hit *Six Feet Under*. Peter joined the cast in the show's fourth season, playing Jimmy, a character series producer Alan Ball described as "sort of the celebrity art student who already has a gallery. . . . Jimmy's very confident, sexy, and charismatic. He knows it and works it." The actor's nine-episode appearance earned him a nomination for a Screen Actors Guild Award.

Peter racked up more experience with short film *Chloe* (2005), dark comedy *Enfants Terribles* (2005), Gen X comedy/drama *The Lather Effect* (2005), and DVD release *Hollow Man 2* with Christian Slater (2006). He played the first blind man to climb Everest in inspirational TV drama *Touch the Top of the World* (2006), and earned an Indie Gathering Award for his return to the L.A. underground in *Arc* (2006).

In 2007, Peter landed a recurring role in another successful TV series — the Golden Globe– and Emmy-winning legal drama *Damages*, starring Glenn Close. Peter appeared in eight episodes as Gregory Malina before his character met an unpleasant end.

The roles kept rolling in: Peter appeared in 2008's *Finding Amanda*, starring Matthew Broderick and Brittany Snow. And 13 years after he made his debut as the devil, the actor had worked his way to the opposite end of the spectrum, and was cast as Jesus in the 2008 short film *Reaper*.

Somewhere between the devil and Jesus falls Dr. Carlisle Cullen, the undead with a conscience. When he heard about the role, Peter went out and bought *Twilight*, which he read the day before his audition for director Catherine Hardwicke. "I couldn't put it down," recalls the actor. "It was fantastic." Peter made it to the final group of actors considered for the role, but lost the part to someone else.

Class act that he is, Peter decided to send the director a gift anyway. Even before the *Twilight* casting call, he had been reading a book on 50 years of vampire moviemaking. He sent the book to Catherine Hardwicke just to say, "Hey, maybe this can inspire you while doing the movie." When the original Carlisle had a scheduling conflict and couldn't take the role, Hardwicke saw the book and called Peter. "I bought my way into *Twilight* for $29.90," he jokes.

For his portrayal of Dr. Carlisle Cullen, Peter went deep, drawing on his first inspiration to act, a young Robert Redford, who, like Carlisle, is "a gentleman, manly, confident, wise-beyond-his-years looking, depth in his eyes, charisma." He also notes, "Carlisle's compassion is very important to me to get across, but also is his need to protect and love for his family. My hope is that parents will be able to identify with Carlisle's struggles with his son Edward." Spoken like a real dad. The most seasoned actor on set, Peter's father role extended beyond the Cullen clan. He told MTV, "We've all bonded, and they all call me Dad."

In between *Twilight* and its sequels, the actor landed another big role, which didn't even require him to take off his lab coat. Peter joined the cast of the Showtime dark comedy *Nurse Jackie*. He plays Dr. Fitch "Coop" Cooper, a doctor with a very inappropriate nervous tic. Despite the fact that both Carlisle and Coop are doctors, "Dr. Carlisle is this calm presence, very knowledgeable, and the patriarch of a family, but Dr. Cooper is just a nervous wreck. [He's] a guy who exudes confidence on the outside, but on the inside, he has no idea what he's doing," says Peter.

Of all his roles, Peter's most important one is as a husband and father. His relationship with Jennie Garth has outlasted most Hollywood unions, and though, as with any relationship, it hasn't always been easy, the family man explains, "Every time we've ridden through the rocky times, our love's gotten deeper." The couple has three daughters: Luca Bella (born June 30, 1997), Lola Ray (born December 6, 2002), and Fiona Eve (born September 30, 2006). Peter often flies home between filming just for quick visits with his family. On a brief break from filming *Eclipse*, he tweeted, "Back in L.A. Going with my daughter on an overnight school camping trip. Guess I haven't spent enough time in the woods. Lol." He also has frequent Skype conversations with his family, even using it to share a long-distance family meal in a pinch: "I'll be eating ramen noodles and they'll be having a wonderful home-cooked meal."

But are Peter's daughters as impressed with their dad's celebrity as legions of *Twilight* fans? He told *People*, "I co-coach my daughter's soccer team and if someone comes over to ask for an autograph, they roll their eyes."

ELIZABETH REASER AS ESME CULLEN

❊ ❊ ❊

Although Elizabeth Reaser has had enormous success in the past few years with attention-getting roles in hits like *Grey's Anatomy* and *Twilight*, like most actors there were times when her audience was considerably more meager. Early in her career, she was part of a London performance that only drew two audience members. But Elizabeth was undeterred, and recalls, "I'd like to think that I worked just as hard in that play, even though there were more people on stage than in the audience."

Elizabeth Ann Reaser was born June 15, 1975, in Bloomfield, Michigan, to parents Karen Davidson and John Reaser. Like many of her fellow actors, Elizabeth recognized her calling from a young age, though she jokingly calls herself at the time "more of a perform-ance artist." She was inspired by the plays she went to see with her parents in New York City, and knew that acting was her vocation when she played Helena in *A Midsummer Night's Dream* at Avondale High School. "In school, I was never good at science or math," she admits. "I always wanted to be an actor, ever since I can remember. I grew up subjecting my family to really bad shows in the living room. It's what I love to do."

Her parents saw her single-minded deter-mination, and gave their daughter their full support. "She knew what she wanted to do, and she had a plan and she just did it," said her mother. "I never doubted that she would do this, because she had no backup — this was it. And I knew she'd succeed at it."

Elizabeth's success started when she was accepted into the prestigious Julliard School, from which she graduated with a Bachelor of Fine Arts in 1999. It didn't take her very long to land a part on a major TV series: in 2000 she appeared in one episode of *The Sopranos*. Her next projects were two well-received films, the Matthew McConaughey drama *Thirteen Conversations About One Thing* and *The Believer*, starring Ryan Gosling, about a Jewish man who becomes a fierce anti-Semite.

More work came her way in 2002; Elizabeth appeared in an episode of *Law & Order: Criminal Intent* and in the film *Emmett's Mark* about a detective who orders a hit on himself. As she pursued film and television

roles, the formally trained actress didn't forget her beginnings on the stage. Between 2000 and 2005, she appeared in productions of *The Hologram Theory*, *Blackbird*, *Closer*, *Stone Cold Dead Serious*, *The Winter's Tale*, and *Top Girls*.

After a string of small parts, Elizabeth landed her first starring role in the 2004 film *Mind the Gap*, which follows five seemingly unrelated people all trying to find happiness. The same year Elizabeth also appeared on two TV series: crime drama *Hack*, and the pilot of the short-lived Fox legal series *The Jury*.

A long dry spell followed for Elizabeth. She had no jobs for nine months, and consid-ered giving up acting for another line of work. But along came the independent film *Sweet Land* and an opportunity for a meaty leading role. Elizabeth plays Inge, a German-born Norwegian immigrant to America just after World War I. As a German and a member of the Socialist party, she's an outcast but taken in by a local farmer, Olaf, despite the scandal of the pair's cohabitation. It was a challenging project, with foreign-language dialogue to master and hard physical labor. The actress remembers, "We were really taking care of ani-mals and riding horses and farming — and freezing. That's why it almost didn't feel like we were doing a movie, because we were just doing it." The film was a modest success, and named one of the top 10 films of 2006 by *Entertainment Weekly* and the *LA Times*, and Elizabeth was given the Jury Award for Best Actress at the Newport Beach Film Festival.

Alongside her indie cinema coup, Elizabeth landed a significant role in a big screen success, the family drama/comedy *The Family Stone*, which also starred big names like Diane Keaton, Sarah Jessica Parker, Dermot

Mulroney, Rachel McAdams, and Luke Wilson. Elizabeth joined another star-studded cast, appearing alongside Ewan McGregor, Ryan Gosling, and Naomi Watts in the mystery *Stay*.

After working on those two major feature films, Elizabeth found her way back to the indie circuit with the 2006 romantic comedy *Puccini for Beginners*. The film debuted at Sundance and co-starred Elizabeth's friend Justin Kirk (*Weeds*). The actress may have played some challenging dramatic roles, but she admitted she found comedy even more difficult. "[Drama's] an easy thing for me to tap into," she confessed. "[Comedy] is more challenging: to work at a different speed, quicker and lighter. It seems easy and fun, but it's more subtle and it's actually harder." And long before a group of Gleeks took television by storm, Elizabeth starred in *The Wedding Weekend* (also released as *Shut Up and Sing*), a film about an a cappella group that reunites at a friend's wedding.

Elizabeth's carefully crafted career led to a main role in the medical series *Saved*. Elizabeth played Alice Alden, a first-year resident in the E.R. The actress described the series as "a character study of people who are living in chaos, trying to save people's lives and scrambling to make sense of their own." Unfortunately, *Saved* only lasted one season.

Elizabeth wasn't through with medical drama, and in 2007, her investment in the genre finally paid dividends when she was cast as Ava/Rebecca, an unidentifiable, disfigured pregnant amnesiac in *Grey's Anatomy*. The role was only supposed to last seven episodes, but Elizabeth's Ava/Rebecca turned into a love interest for hot-shot doc Alex Karev. She ended up guest-starring on the series for 17

episodes — longer than her own show had lasted! Elizabeth also won the hearts of fans and critics alike, and was nominated for an Emmy, a Screen Actors Guild Award, and a Prism Award. During her time on *Grey's*, Elizabeth also appeared in *Purple Violets*, a relationship comedy, which had the distinction of being the first movie ever released directly on iTunes.

Next up for Elizabeth was another smaller film . . . a project just for the fans: Catherine Hardwicke's *Twilight*. Elizabeth was cast as Esme, wife to Dr. Carlisle and surrogate mother to Edward, Alice, Jasper, Emmett, and Rosalie. Elizabeth hasn't been shy about admitting she

thinks she is nothing like her character. She told MTV: "It's interesting to me that I get cast as mothers and really maternal, sweet, nice people. . . . Maybe I have a vulnerability or something; maybe that's what it is. But other than that, I don't relate to this type of character. She's so good and lovely, and it definitely makes me [a better person]. When I'm working, and I'm always trying to see people in their best light, it makes me a more generous person to play Esme, because I don't feel that." Reaser would have cast Bryce Dallas Howard in the role. Said Elizabeth, "She's so lovely and beautiful and kind and good. I nominate her to play Esme Cullen." But that actress would replace Rachelle Lefevre as Victoria in *Eclipse*. There is one thing Reaser does have in common with her character: her vamp counterpart is a "vegetarian," while Elizabeth is a vegan.

Despite her increased exposure from the international film sensation, Elizabeth's life and career haven't been dramatically transformed. "I don't feel like anything has changed, believe it or not. I get recognized a little bit more, but that's it. I feel like my life is just as boring as ever," she jokes. "I've never been in a movie that anyone's really seen so that's nice. What's also cool about it is that I love all of these actors so we have a good time together. It's a party. We have fun."

In 2008, Elizabeth got another shot at her own series. This time it was *The Ex-List*, an adaptation from an Israeli sitcom about a woman who has a psychic tell her she has already met the love of her life, spurring her to comb through her past to find him.

Elizabeth's character is coincidentally named Bella, and seems to have more than a name in common with her vamp-loving counterpart. Elizabeth explained the appeal of her *Ex-List* character: "What I love about Bella is her unapologetic search to fall in love. What's amazing to me about that is I feel like, in this day and age, if you're a woman and you're successful and you're strong, you're not supposed to want a man and you're supposed to just be cool being alone all the time. I don't feel that way. I want to be with someone. And so, what I love about the show is that it's completely unapologetic in that quest to find love and connection." Unfortunately for Elizabeth, this was her second strike with a television series; with low ratings and mixed reviews, *The Ex-List* was canceled before all its episodes had aired.

But Elizabeth had other projects on the go, including *New Moon* and *Eclipse* as well as what she calls "a really fun, cool little film," *Against the Current*, co-starring Joseph Fiennes and reuniting her with pal Justin Kirk. Despite some setbacks Elizabeth is living her dream, having gone from her Michigan living room to film premieres across the globe. Elizabeth's father generously appraised his daughter. "We're all happy that she enjoys what she does, because that's so important," he said. "[But] her success, I think, is secondary to the fact that she just is a wonderful person and committed to just making everybody around her a little bit better, and that's what we love so much about her." It seems like Elizabeth may have more in common with Esme than she thinks.

The Nomads

CAM GIGANDET
AS JAMES

❄ ❄ ❄

When Cam Joslin Gigandet hightailed it from his hometown of Auburn, Washington, to L.A. just after graduating high school, he wasn't a Hollywood hopeful, he just didn't want to be a small town boy for life. He told *Interview*, "I left on a whim and was hanging around for a couple months before someone said, 'You should try acting.' Once I actually went, I loved it, and I kind of knew in that moment that's what I wanted to do."

Born August 16, 1982, in Tacoma, the young actor with golden boy looks didn't have to wait long for Hollywood to notice him. His first job was in an independent short film, followed by a role on *CSI*. Cam went on to nab recurring roles in legendary soap *The Young and the Restless*, WB drama *Jack & Bobby*, and, most memorably, in *The O.C.* as bad boy Kevin Volchok. Pre-*Twilight*, he also appeared in golf comedy *Who's Your Caddy?* (2007), and in *Never Back Down* (2008) as fight-club bully Ryan McCarthy (whose brawling earned him an MTV Movie Award for Best Fight).

Cam had actually read *Twilight* before Summit was officially casting. Knowing it would one day become a movie, he was careful to read it conspicuously on the set of *Never Back Down*, which was also a Summit production. Apparently it worked out, because Cam made the cut, although he was originally slated to play Emmett Cullen. He recalls, "When I read the book, I thought, if this becomes a movie, I have to be James." And so Cam went from bearish big bro to bloodthirsty tracker, a role more in line with his history of villainous roles. Cam did clarify to MTV, "All the bad guys that I've played, they're justifiably bad — they have their reasons. It's been important to me." For him, the best part of playing James wasn't his evil motivations, but "playing with the idea of immortality, and how it is both good and bad. And his fears were really intriguing to me." Asked what could explain the widespread fascination with vampires, Cam replied, "Anything — a destination, a person — that has some mystery around it becomes exciting and attractive. And with vampires, you have this secret world on top of their raw sexual power and intensity. The combination of those things is extremely captivating."

Unfortunately, by choosing James over Emmett, Cam was also passing on the *Twilight* sequels. But the vamp drama still added a little sparkle to his career, and his popularity grew when he took home a Teen Choice Award for Choice Movie Villain, and Choice Movie Rumble for his ballet-studio brawl with Robert Pattinson.

On April 14, 2009, Cam became a dad to Everleigh Rae Gigandet, his first child with girlfriend Dominique Geisendorff. Expecting a child may have been a little eerie for Cam who appeared in horror flick *The Unborn* (2009) about an unborn baby with a vengeance, while he awaited his daughter's arrival. Work was steady for Cam post-*Twilight*: sci-fi flick *Pandorum* opposite Dennis Quaid, thrillers *Kerosene Cowboys* and *The Roommate* (with Leighton Meester), and high school comedy *Easy A*. In vampire-western *Priest*, Cam switched sides to play the vampire-hunting sheriff, and he'll "Play it again, Cam,"

as a pianist in Christina Aguilera's film debut, *Burlesque*. He calls the musical "a very sexy, sexy movie." As if there were any doubt.

RACHELLE LEFEVRE
AS VICTORIA

❋ ❋ ❋

It's a story fit for Hollywood: Rachelle Lefevre was working as a waitress at Montreal sushi bar Kaizen, telling a customer how she wanted to be an actress, when she was overheard by a regular who had a casting-director friend. That casting director hooked her up with her first role, which turned out to be a regular part on the *Buffy*-esque werewolf drama *Big Wolf on Campus*. As cheerleader Stacey Hanson, Rachelle was "always the damsel in distress," but the lighthearted horror series had a big impact on her career, just as another supernatural franchise would nearly a decade later, when she'd be back to running with werewolves, this time as their sworn enemy.

Rachelle Marie Lefevre was born February 1, 1979, in Montreal, Quebec, and was raised there along with her three sisters. She attended Centennial High School, then Dawson College, before beginning a degree at McGill University, which she would abandon in favor of acting.

For almost a decade after *Big Wolf on Campus*, Rachelle would find piece work in TV movies and shows such as *Bones*, *Veronica Mars*, *How I Met Your Mother*, *CSI*, *The Closer*, and *Boston Legal*. She even landed recurring roles on the short-lived Fox sitcom *Life on a Stick*, ABC dramedy *What About Brian?*, and 1970s suburban drama *Swingtown*. Her film credits

include star-studded thriller *Confessions of a Dangerous Mind* (2002), *Head in the Clouds* (with Charlize Theron and Penelope Cruz, 2004), and the award-winning book adaptation *Fugitive Pieces* (2007).

Then Rachelle's agent called about a part in another low-budget film called *Twilight*. The actress immediately went out to buy the book, and devoured it in two and a half days. Fortunately, "not only was Victoria the role I had the audition for, but it was also the role that when I was reading the book, I was really attracted to and wanted to play." Rachelle desperately wanted the part, for three reasons: first, she loved vampires. At age 14, when she finished reading Bram Stoker's *Dracula*, she recalls, "I read the last page, closed the back cover, and then said, 'No, not enough,' and flipped the book over and started reading it again." Second, she was a big fan of Catherine Hardwicke's previous work. In fact, she demonstrated not only her dedication to the part, but her vampire knowledge, with a three-page personal letter to the director explaining why she should get the part. Rachelle told MTV, "Most of it was about how I thought that vampires were basically the best metaphor for human anxiety and questions about being alive. I also said I wanted to do something that appeals to both a younger and an older audience." And third, she knew there was potential for sequels, which would mean steady work and a chance to develop her character over time.

Whether it was the letter or her audition, the red-headed actress landed the role of fiery huntress Victoria. Rachelle describes Victoria as "a woman who is half-cat and is extremely

THE twilight TOUR
11/10 -11/15/08

SAN FRANCISCO
SEATTLE
DALLAS
DENVER
CHICAGO
PHOENIX
PHILADELPHIA

MINNEAPOLIS
WA

powerful and enjoys her power." To prepare for the role as the blood-thirsty villain, Rachelle read all the books, and then spent some time trying to create a relatable backstory for her character. She wanted to make sure her portrayal wasn't all evil "mustache-twirling," and explained, "I spent a lot of time making sure that it was a fun and sort of evil portrayal but also an honest one."

When *Twilight* turned out to be a sensation all over the world, Rachelle knew she'd caught the big break she'd been waiting for. She enthused, "This is by far the biggest thing I've ever been a part of. I've had pretty good luck with TV but I'm hoping this opens some movie doors for me."

It certainly did. She was back as Victoria in the *New Moon* sequel, which proved an even bigger hit than the first installment; in public appearances she was regularly greeted by thousands of fans. But her Twilight romance took an abrupt turn when she was infamously fired from *Eclipse* over a scheduling conflict. The actress released a statement saying, "I was stunned by Summit's decision to recast the role of Victoria for *Eclipse*. . . . Given the length of filming for *Eclipse*, never did I fathom I would lose the role over a 10-day overlap." The conflict came from Rachelle's role in a film adaptation of the award-winning Canadian novel *Barney's Version*, in which she would play Barney's first wife Clara. Summit released their own statement, saying Rachelle had kept the other engagement from them until the last minute, and insisting, "It is not about a 10-day overlap, but instead about the fact that *The Twilight Saga: Eclipse* is an ensemble production that has to accommodate the schedules of numerous actors while respecting the established creative vision of the filmmaker and most importantly the story." The Twitterverse lit up with a campaign to bring back Rachelle, who had been replaced by Bryce Dallas Howard. But to no avail. Nevertheless, Rachelle was grateful to her fans, and announced on Twitter, "I am so touched by all your responses and feel incredibly blessed to have fans like you. . . . From the bottom of my heart: thank you."

It was a heartbreaking setback, but Rachelle still had her role in *Barney's Version* alongside Dustin Hoffman and Paul Giamatti, and she knew the part as emotional artist Clara was "one of those roles that comes along maybe once or twice in a career." And despite the loss of one opportunity, a new diverse array of roles presented themselves. In 2010 she'll also play press secretary Emily Miller in the political thriller *Casino Jack* opposite Kevin Spacey, she replaced Brittany Murphy as the lead in thriller *The Caller*, and she's been tapped for *VK*, a period piece starring Adrien Brody, about the 18th century Hungarian inventor of a chess-playing machine. It's exactly the direction the actress would like her career to go: "I'm always looking to do things that are really different from each other; I like stepping out of my comfort zone."

It was a rocky road for the Canadian actress, but she's come a long way from waiting tables, and she knows it. Says Rachelle, "I'm so grateful to be doing what I'm doing. Whatever happens along the way, you just shake it off and continue to forge ahead with what you love."

At Comic-Con in 2008 (L-R): Edi, Cam, Stephenie, Rob, Catherine, Kristen, Taylor, and Rachelle.

EDI GATHEGI
AS LAURENT

❋ ❋ ❋

While attending University of California Santa Barbara, Edi Mue Gathegi never considered a career as an actor. He wanted to play basketball, but while training with his teammates, he blew out his knee, and his basketball career was officially over. Looking, as he says, "to break up the monotony of depression," and for an easy class, Edi enrolled in an acting course and fell in love with it. He auditioned for the U.C. Santa Barbara conservatory program, and got in. The Kenyan-born

actor then auditioned for the prestigious Tisch graduate program at NYU, and was accepted. U.C. Santa Barbara had given him a good foundation, but he realized, "I had the drive and the passion and I loved it, but I honestly wasn't good enough to come out to L.A. and make it happen."

With a prestigious graduate degree under his belt, Edi was ready to take on Hollywood. His first role was as a Haitian cabbie in action thriller *Crank* about a professional assassin who has been injected with a poison that is lethal if his heart rate drops. He also appeared on *Lincoln Heights* and *Veronica Mars*, and in the 2007 films *Gone Baby Gone*, *The Fifth Patient*, and *Death Sentence*. But Edi really made his mark as Dr. Jeffrey "Big Love" Cole on *House*, a Mormon doctor in House's *Survivor*-style competition to determine who would comprise his new team. It was Edi's first steady role and he says, "I loved it. I felt secure, I had a job, had a routine and I was getting to act with these wonderful actors." Unfortunately Dr. Cole was fired from the team, but, like Edi's knee injury, it turned out to be another blessing in disguise.

As he was looking for work, a casting director friend pointed him toward the *Twilight* project. After his first audition for nomadic vampire Laurent, Edi was still a little unsure about the role, but reading the books changed his mind. He told the *LA Times*, "I've read them all. *Breaking Dawn*? I finished that in two days. I have to tell you, every time I finished one of them, a little piece of me died. I'd become invested in that world. I really felt sad." He has nothing but admiration for Stephenie Meyer, who he didn't see while filming but met at a Comic-Con dinner when they were seated next to one another. They ended up bonding over Mormonism, since Edi had played a Mormon on *House*. It was a great evening for the actor, who admits, "I monopolized her time, really, but I was just so excited. She's a doll."

The other thing that changed his mind about the role was his audition with Catherine Hardwicke. Says Edi, "During the auditions, I had a blast with Catherine. Her energy and enthusiasm won me over. In Hollywood, you don't have a lot of awesome audition experiences, but she and I just clicked." There was a slight problem though. There were no explic-itly African-American characters in *Twilight*, and Laurent was described as "olive-skinned." But Edi addressed the situation cleverly, saying, "Listen, she describes this character as being olive-toned. But there are many different types of olives. Black olives anyone?" The issue was officially put to rest.

Edi resists categorizing Laurent as an evil vampire just because he gives in to his natural blood-drinking impulses. He calls him "not just all bad, but he's not completely good." Aside from reading the books, Edi's preparation for the role included learning as much French as he could so he could do a convincing accent. "I just sort of immersed myself in all things French. I even tried to get myself a French girlfriend, but that didn't work out," he joked to *Vanity Fair*. He also dedicated himself to getting buff for his mostly shirtless role, training with Taylor Lautner. He praises Taylor's single-minded dedication: "He does not let up. I ask, 'What do we do?' [and he would reply,] 'Everything! The whole routine.'"

After *Twilight* wrapped, Edi was able to sneak in another film before he had to reprise his role as Laurent in *New Moon*. He played Deputy Martin, one of many potential suspects in the slasher film remake *My Bloody Valentine*, released in January 2009 to positive reviews. He also expanded his paranormal repertoire playing a ghost in *This Is Not a Movie*, and is back on TV in the pilot for *Operating Instructions*. Unfortunately, since Laurent doesn't survive his wolf encounter in *New Moon*, there will be no more Twilight sequels for Edi, though he joked, "I am trying to commission Stephenie Meyer to write the Laurent chronicles."

chapter 10

Forks
Folks

BILLY BURKE
AS CHARLIE SWAN

❄ ❄ ❄

Washington-native Billy Burke knew what kind of career he wanted pretty early in life: "As soon as I was old enough to comprehend that there was an actual job where you get paid to goof off most the time, I began to gear everything toward having that job." After almost 20 years in the business, William Albert Burke has a long résumé to his credit. He's appeared on a number of major television shows such as *Party of Five*, *Star Trek: Deep Space Nine*, *Gilmore Girls*, *Wonderland*, *Law & Order*, and *Fringe*, and has the unfortunate claim to fame of having shot 10 failed pilots. He's best known in the television world as Gary Matheson on the hit action series *24*. He's also landed roles in numerous movies, such as *Along Came a Spider*, *Ladder 49*, *Untraceable*, and *Feast of Love*.

Billy was familiar with playing cops from his TV work, and when it came time to audition for the role of Chief Swan, he knew it'd be a good fit because, he admits, "I tend to gravitate toward characters that carry their damage in their hip pocket." He explains, "I consider Charlie to be a guy placed in the middle of a miasma [unpleasant situation] that he's unaware of. All he wants to do is reconnect with his daughter."

Screenwriter Melissa Rosenberg lavished high praise on Billy Burke's portrayal of the Forks Police chief, which brought her unexpressed impression of the character to the screen. She told the *LA Times*, "Billy Burke I thought was just incredible. I wasn't sure at first, because I didn't really have an actor in mind while I was writing Charlie, but he so beautifully embodied that relationship with Bella. He's one that really stands out for me."

Shortly after he finished playing dad to Bella Swan in *Twilight*, Billy Burke became a dad in real life, when he welcomed daughter Bluesy LaRue into the world. It gave him new perspective on the father–daughter bond when it was time to film *New Moon*. He explains, "I just realized that when you're a father, there is no better word in the English language than the word 'daddy' spoken by your daughter. I mean it kills you, every single time. I guess during the second and third movies, I did have a better appreciation for Charlie's relationship with Bella."

Billy will star in the musical *Baby O*, drama *Ticket Out*, thriller *Shadow Play*, and comedy/drama *Highland Park*. And when Bluesy was only a few months old, the new dad combined work with family time, sharing the screen in indie thriller *Luster* with his daughter and wife, Pollyanna Rose.

ANNA KENDRICK
AS JESSICA STANLEY

❄ ❄ ❄

Born August 9,1985, Anna Kendrick has never been interested in schoolyard drama like her *Twilight* character Jessica Stanley; she knew from a young age that she wanted her drama to take place on stage. She calls herself "one of those hyperactive kids who wanted to jump around and sing and dance and scream and be on stage." Her dedicated parents drove her back and forth from their Portland, Maine, home to New York City so she could audition for more than community productions. She signed with her first agent at age 11, and exploded into professional acting with a role as Dinah in the Broadway musical *High Society*, a role that would earn her a Theatre World Award and nominations for both a Tony and a Drama Desk Award. She continued her stage work playing Fredrika in the New York City Opera's *A Little Night Music*. In 2003 she demonstrated her vocal talents to filmgoers in the musical comedy *Camp*, and went on to impress critics as a sharp-tongued debater in 2007's *Rocket Science*. Seeing her in this role inspired director Jason Reitman to write a part for her in *Up in the Air*, a performance that

would earn her a Golden Globe and an Oscar nomination. When she auditioned for the role, the director praised, "She came in and read against every great actress of her generation, and she just crushed it." Though she was ill for her *Twilight* audition, she still got the part, and enjoyed playing Bella's annoyingly insecure friend. "She's a little pathetic, and she's kind of a brat. But she's really fun to play," says Anna. The up-and-comer's most recent projects include *The Mark Pease Experience* (with Jason Schwartzman and Ben Stiller) and *Scott Pilgrim vs. The World* (with Michael Cera).

MICHAEL WELCH
AS MIKE NEWTON

❋ ❋ ❋

Out of all the *Twilight* cast members, Michael Alan Welch certainly has the most socks. After he mentioned to the Twilight Lexicon that he was on a road trip and running low on socks, fans lent a hand, sending him hundreds of pairs. But it wasn't all socks and stardom from the beginning for Michael Welch. The actor, born July 25, 1987, in L.A., has been hard at work since age 10, working on over 20 films and on over 30 TV shows including *CSI*, *Malcolm in the Middle*, *Frasier*, *7th Heaven*, and the critically acclaimed *Joan of Arcadia*, playing the younger brother to Joan. Michael received two Young Artist Awards for his work on *Joan of Arcadia* and *Star Trek: Insurrection*. Michael originally auditioned for Edward, but didn't quite fit the part of the hauntingly handsome vamp, and a mix-and-match audition found him better suited to playing the lovelorn highschooler Mike

Newton. Describing his character in the Twilight Saga, the actor fell back on the wisdom of *Family Guy*'s Peter: "Not quite the nerd, not quite the hunk — Shia LaBeouf!" Though his part in the Twilight films was somewhat small, the actor's lined up enough work to rival Shia LaBeouf, starring in dramas *Lost Dream* and *Rough Hustle*, and thriller *Unrequited* all in 2010.

CHRISTIAN SERRATOS
AS ANGELA WEBER

❋ ❋ ❋

Born September 21, 1990, Christian Serratos started acting in front of the television, mimicking the lines of the actresses on screen. By age 14, the avid singer, dancer, and figure skater appeared on screen instead of in front of it with roles in the short film *Mrs. Marshall*, and then in a recurring role on *Ned's Declassified School Survival Guide* as Ned's crush Suzie Crabgrass. She went on to star in TV movie *Cow Belles* and appeared in *Zoey 101*, *Hannah Montana*, and *7th Heaven*. When Christian heard that the Twilight Saga was being turned into movies, she rushed out to buy the books and tore through them. She initially auditioned to play Jessica, but was thrilled when she got the chance to try out for Angela, since she really related to the dependable photographer. Though Angela isn't a scene stealer, Christian argues, "I keep feeling like there is more to her. Something that isn't visible." Christian relates to the vegetarian vamps, since she's a passionate advocate for animal rights and vegetarianism in real life. She was even willing to bare all for the cause,

and in 2009, she appeared nude in PETA's "I'd Rather Go Naked Than Wear Fur" campaign.

JUSTIN CHON
AS ERIC YORKIE

❋ ❋ ❋

Justin Jitae Chon has acting in his blood; his father was a successful actor in South Korea. After immigrating to America, where Justin was born on May 29, 1981, his father gave up acting and started a career in retail. Justin grew up thinking he'd like to follow in his dad's footsteps, but he noticed that there were very few Asian actors on TV. He remembers, "By the time I reached college, I saw more Asian faces on TV. I thought, 'Hey, maybe I can do this.'" But Justin pursued his studies, and graduated from college with a bachelor's in business administration from the University of Southern California. He'd been taking twice-weekly drama classes during his degree, and decided he'd give acting a shot for two years. After starting off with a lot of unpaid work, he landed a commercial with T-Mobile, and finally a guest spot on the WB's *Jack & Bobby* in 2005. A few small movie roles and an appearance on *The O.C.* followed, but Justin's big break was when he was cast as Jordan's best friend Tony Lee on the Nickelodeon sitcom *Just Jordan*. But even with a recurring role on a popular teen sitcom, Justin wasn't prepared for the fandom that came with being a part of the Twilight screen scene. Justin was cast as Forks High School student Eric Yorkie, who he describes as a "very energetic, optimistic, overachieving guy who wants to fit in and be cool with everyone at school." Since *Twilight*, Justin's major accomplishment has been as part of the star-studded cast in the 2009 independent drama *Crossing Over*. The young actor is still amazed at his success, and admits, "In the beginning I never thought I could do it, and even now, while I'm passionate about acting, I'm not 100 percent confident in my work. I still have trouble believing that people would want to hire me."

chapter 11

Enough for Forever

"I get to kiss Edward Cullen."

– Kristen on why it's great
to play Bella Swan

With actors cast and a crew assembled, the production of *Twilight* sped ahead, with principal photography beginning in March 2008 for a scheduled 45 days. Hardwicke and her team faced a challenging shoot on a tight timeline — could they best the fickle and fierce Oregon weather, create believable special effects for the vampires' speed and sparkle, and capture the intense and emotional journey of Edward and Bella's romance?

Ashley, Kellan, Nikki, Jackson, and Taylor at a stop on the *Twilight* Hot Topic tour.

While filming *Twilight*, Rob tried to keep himself isolated, not talking unnecessarily so his performance as Edward would have the awkwardness of someone not used to conversing. The actor frequented the legendary Powell's Books in Portland, which he calls the most amazing bookshop, and read a lot, in particular Martin Amis and Virgil's *Doomed Love*. The latter he passed on to Kristen Stewart for "inspiration" (and jokes that she didn't even read it). On working with Kristen, Pattinson said, "We definitely had a strange dynamic. Like, I mean, at the beginning I was intimidated by her but at the same time was like, 'You're younger than me you can't intimidate me,' [laughs] so you're just fighting against yourself the whole time, which I guess kind of worked for it." Describing Kristen as someone with a "fierceness," Robert says, "there's an anger behind her quietness," which unsettled the actor when they first were getting to know one another. As filming progressed, the two fell into a close working relationship. "Literally every single scene is really intense and it became like a bubble, separate from the cast and separate from other people and stuff, which I guess was the whole point in the movie," says Rob.

Kristen had known Rob was the man to play Edward as soon as he auditioned. "He's very responsive — he sees and he listens — and that's very important, that you're not acting in a scene by yourself," said Kristen of her co-star. Interviewed by MTV while on the set of *Twilight*, Kristen revealed that she and Rob prepared for their roles by pouring over the script at her living-room table during pre-production. She also suggested that 1972's racy NC17-rated *Last Tango in Paris* was the movie that the two "bonded" over, prompting Pattinson to joke that they were basing Bella and Edward's relationship on the film's twisted dynamic. From these first interviews and over the course of the press tour that hyped *Twilight*'s release, it became apparent to fans that the actors portraying Edward and Bella weren't going to spout the same canned, boring answers over and over again. Their playfulness, irreverence, and delight in absurd responses make Kristen-and-Rob interviews more fun to watch than most actors'.

But that goofiness didn't indicate a lack of seriousness about their characters. Kristen knew that even though Rob was getting a lot of fan attention, it was through her character that audience members enter the world of *Twilight*. "I sort of play the eyes of the story, you experience everything through Bella, and I play a pretty logical girl, she's pretty normal, she's very intense. A lot of love stories start out like the girl is searching for something, she needs to be fulfilled and something's missing. [But Bella is] very okay with her situation, and she gets swept into something that is entirely, um, fantastical and larger than her." Kristen was pleased that she would be once again portraying a strong, complicated character, and also enjoyed the now-rare approach Hardwicke and her team took to filming: they tried to do as much of the special effects in-camera, rather than rely on green screens and CGI. Partly due to their small budget but also an artistic choice, Hardwicke, who's known for a cinéma-vérité style, argued, "If you just do it for real, if you can, it's gonna look better." That meant Kristen spent days in a harness attached to Rob as they filmed the "spider monkey" scenes, with stunt performers

Replicating the actual Forks, WA, signs; serving berry cobbler at the diner, an item plucked from an actual Forks menu . . . just a couple of the many tiny details that made the fantastical world of *Twilight* realistic. Another was Charlie's beer of choice. Named after Mount Rainier, Rainier beer (a.k.a. "Vitamin R") was originally made in a Seattle brewery and is popular in the Pacific Northwest.

standing in to film the stunning helicopter shot that circles the pair perched in a tree high above the ground.

Another ongoing challenge for the *Twilight* crew was the weather in Portland. "We had to jump around; every five minutes the weather changed," said Kristen of the elements' control over the production. Normally a nice sunny day is a good thing for filming outside, but for *Twilight* a sunny day meant the crew had to

When you can live forever,
what do you live for?

> "The barometer I use is the Stephenie Meyer [set] visits, and the fact that she's been so thrilled with everything she's seen has been the strongest vote of confidence, feeling that we're doing the right thing and delivering to her audience what she so effectively delivered in book form."
>
> — producer Greg Mooradian
> during *Twilight* principal photography

move indoors to shoot scenes; errant sunbeams couldn't hit a vampire or else they'd have to sparkle! Realizing the immense interest in every detail of how the film was made — like how that vampire sparkle effect was achieved — Little, Brown published two companion volumes to the film: *Twilight: The Complete Illustrated Movie Companion* by Mark Cotta Vaz, which overviews the filmmaking process, interviews the key production members, and is filled with stunning on-set photos and production stills; and Catherine Hardwicke's *Twilight Director's Notebook: The Story of How We Made the Movie Based on the Novel by Stephenie Meyer*, which offers a rare glimpse into a director's process and is filled with doodles, photos, insider information, and Hardwicke's unique perspective.

Fans didn't wait for those books to be published before they set into analyzing the film adaptation. Long before *Twilight*'s release, anticipation was high and every tidbit of information, still released, or fan photo taken of the set was devoured. The official kick-off to the promotion for the film took place at San Diego Comic-Con in July 2008 where Twilighters "took over" the convention to see Stephenie Meyer, Catherine Hardwicke, and the cast. The panel was greeted with a packed hall of enthusiastic, screaming fans who were only egged on by answers like Rob Pattinson's when asked why he took on the role of Edward: "I just wanted to play the hottest vampire on Earth. He's so hot it hurts me. It hurts me to think about myself."

On November 21, the wait was over. In its opening weekend, the film more than earned its estimated budget of $37 million, grossing nearly $70 million. Female-focused movies have a history of underperforming at the box office, but *Twilight* fans proved that a film written by a woman, adapted from a female novelist's book, directed by a woman, and centered on a teenage girl could smash all expectations. The critical response was mixed, with most reviewers opining that this was a film for fans of Stephenie Meyer and not for fans of vampire movies. The *New York Times* called it "a deeply sincere, outright goofy vampire romance" while *Entertainment Weekly* praised the casting choices of Stewart and Pattinson as well as Hardwicke as director, because she "treats teen confusion without a trace of condescension." The response to the

A sly wink to the company that had the good sense to publish *Twilight* was included in the film adaptation. When Bella finds the Quileute legend book online, the list of retailers in the margin includes Little, Brown.

film paralleled the response to Meyer's novels: the audience loved it, the haters found lots of material to poke fun of, and entertainment writers spilled ink marveling at its success. A devoted fan of the book, Kristen Stewart was happy with the adaptation, saying, "All of the iconic scenes are in the movie, and the essence and the feeling." And Stephenie Meyer felt the same way as her on-screen Bella. Though she'd been involved in the entire process, it was hard to tell how the movie would turn out in the end. But watching a rough cut, she felt "so involved" that she didn't make one note for improvement, and experienced the same range of emotions as when reading *Twilight*. Stephenie said she came away with the "same sense of 'This is complicated, but hopeful.'"

With the film's box-office success, it was inevitable that Summit Entertainment would also adapt *New Moon* for the screen. While they awaited the sequel, *Twilight* fans poured over the film, memorizing the lines, reliving favorite moments, discussing Easter eggs (like Stephenie's cameo in the diner or the shot that replicated the *Twilight* cover in the cafeteria), pointing out bloopers, and cataloguing the changes from the book to the script. The film received a wealth of award nominations and won Best Movie, Best Female Performance (Kristen Stewart), Breakthrough Performance Male (Rob Pattinson), Best Kiss (Kristen and Rob), and Best Fight (Rob vs. Cam Gigandet) at the MTV Movie Awards; Best Fantasy Movie, Actress (Kristen), and Actor (Rob), and Best Breakout Performance (Taylor Lautner) at the Scream Awards; and at the Teen Choice Awards won Choice Movie: Drama, Movie: Romance, Movie Actor: Drama (Rob), Movie Actress: Drama (Kristen), Movie Villain (Cam), Movie: Fresh Face Female (Ashley Greene), Movie: Fresh Face Male (Taylor Lautner), Movie Rumble (Rob vs. Cam), Movie Liplock (Kristen and Rob), and Music Soundtrack.

THE SOUNDTRACK

The majority of books adapted for film don't come with a playlist suggested by the author, but like most things *Twilight*, Stephenie Meyer created the exception to the rule. Heavily influenced and inspired by music while writing, Stephenie shared the names of those songs and artists with her readers. When it came time to put together the soundtrack to the film, Catherine Hardwicke and music supervisor Alex Patsavas had a wealth of suggestions at their fingertips. Head of her own company, Chop Shop Music Supervision, Patsavas first worked on soundtracks to films (*Happy, Texas*; *Gun Shy*) before focusing primarily on TV

FILMING LOCATIONS

Not only has the real Forks, Washington, become a hot tourist spot since Twilighters began touring the locations Stephenie Meyer mentioned in her book series, but so have Portland and towns like Vernonia and St. Helens, Oregon, which stood in for Forks on screen. Here are a few of the key spots where *Twilight* filmed.

The Swan residence: The Swans may live in Forks, but the house where both the interior and exterior scenes were filmed is a private residence at 184 S. 6th Street in St. Helens, Oregon. A sign on the lawn asks *Twilight* fans to please take photos from across the street.

The Cullen home: Referred to as the "Nike House" after it was purchased by a Nike executive, this architectural wonder at 3333 NW Quimby Street in Portland played house to the vegetarian vamps in *Twilight*. Though this private home is difficult for fans to see much of from the public road, it does have its own website featuring tons of beautiful photographs (3333q.com).

The Bloated Toad: In Meyer's novel, the restaurant where Bella and Edward dine is La Bella Italia, an actual restaurant in Port Angeles. Since *Twilight* filmed elsewhere, the locations team made up the much-less-romantically named "Bloated Toad" and filmed at a private residence (330 S. 1st Street) in St. Helens.

The Thunderbird and Whale Bookstore: In a deviation from the novel, Bella actually enters the Port Angeles bookstore in the film, buying the book on Quileute legends from fictional store the Thunderbird and Whale. The exterior of the shop was filmed in St. Helens at a building that houses a law office (260 S. 2nd Street).

The dress shop: The scene where Jessica and Angela try on dresses was filmed in St. Helens' Angel Hair Salon (251 S. 1st Street), and the salon now proudly displays Catherine Hardwicke's director's chair.

Forks High prom: The Monte Carlo-themed prom was filmed at The View Point Inn (40301 E. Larch Mountain Road) in Corbett, Oregon. The real-life hotel posted photos from the shoot of Robert and Kristen in their prom gear on TheViewPointInn.com, and now hosts Twilight-themed events and serves mushroom ravioli in its restaurant.

series. Starting with *Roswell*, Alex has gone on to music supervise *Carnivale*, *Boston Public*, *Fastlane*, *Private Practice*, *Chuck*, *Without a Trace*, *Rescue Me*, *Mad Men*, *Supernatural*, *Numb3rs*, *Grey's Anatomy*, *The O.C.*, and *Gossip Girl*. In 2007, Alex formed a music label named after her company, Chop Shop Records, and landed a deal with Atlantic Records.

It wasn't only Stephenie Meyer whose influence could be heard in the final track listing (with bands like Muse, Linkin Park, and Collective Soul featured) or Rob Pattinson who could literally be heard on the soundtrack; Kristen Stewart also put her two cents in, sug-

gesting Iron & Wine's "Flightless Bird, American Mouth" for the song Edward and Bella dance to in the gazebo during the intense final moments of the film. The lead single on the soundtrack, "Decode," came from Tennessee's Paramore (pictured above). Lead singer Hayley Williams had read *Twilight*, loved it, and wanted to be a part of the soundtrack. Said the vocalist, "I was calling anyone and everyone I could to figure out how we could be a part of it." Knowing that there was serious crossover between fans of her band and those of the Twilight Saga, she wrote the lyrics to "Decode" and sent the nearly finished song to

SONG BY SCENE
THE TWILIGHT SOUNDTRACK

1. "Supermassive Black Hole," Muse
   The Cullens introduce Bella to vampire baseball.

2. "Decode," Paramore
   The lead single off the soundtrack doesn't appear in the film until the end credits.

3. "Full Moon," The Black Ghosts
   Bella leaves Phoenix and heads for Forks.

4. "Leave Out All the Rest," Linkin Park
   End credits.

5. "Spotlight (Twilight Mix)," Mute Math
   Edward and Bella arrive at Forks High – officially a couple.

6. "Go All the Way (Into the Twilight)," Perry Farrell
   Bella and Edward at prom.

7. "Tremble for My Beloved," Collective Soul
   Edward and Bella exchange a meaningful look after he saves her from being crushed by Tyler's van.

8. "I Caught Myself," Paramore
   Jessica and Angela try on dresses while Bella feigns interest.

9. "Eyes on Fire," Blue Foundation
   After talking to Renée on the phone, Bella thinks about confronting Edward.

10. "Never Think," Rob Pattinson
    Edward reveals his ability to read minds as Bella eats mushroom ravioli in Port Angeles.

11. "Flightless Bird, American Mouth," Iron & Wine
    In the gazebo, Bella and Edward dance; she asks him to turn her into a vampire.

12. "Bella's Lullaby," Carter Burwell
    The theme for Bella and Edward; he plays it for her on the piano.
    (bonus) "Let Me Sign," Rob Pattinson
    Edward sucks the venom out of Bella.
    (bonus) "La Traviata," (Verdi) Royal Philharmonic Orchestra
    Bella meets the Cullens at their home.
    (bonus) "Clair de Lune," (Debussy) The APM Orchestra
    In Edward's bedroom for the first time, Bella recognizes the music on his stereo.

Hardwicke, who loved it and asked them to contribute a second song ("I Caught Myself").

On November 4, 2008, the *Twilight Original Motion Picture Soundtrack* was released on Chop Shop Records and debuted at the top of the Billboard 200. In addition to being enthusiastically received by fans, the album won a 2009 American Music Award for Best Soundtrack, and was nominated for two Grammys (for Best Compilation Soundtrack Album and Best Song Written for Motion Picture, Television or Other Visual Media for "Decode"). The score to the film, by accomplished composer Carter Burwell (*Conspiracy Theory, Where the Wild Things Are*), was released to eager Twilighters digitally on November 25 and on CD December 8. The score was praised by *Film Music* for its ability to "veer from the melancholy to the savage," and for its "ethereal samples that cast a truly magical spell over the dew-speckled trees and vampire skin."

chapter 12

New Moon Rises

"What if true love left you? Not some ordinary high school romance, not some random jock boyfriend, not anyone at all replaceable. True love. The real deal." That's the question Stephenie Meyer set out to answer for Bella in *New Moon*, and she had carefully laid the groundwork for the intensity of her heroine's heartbreak in *Twilight*.

Throughout the Twilight Saga, Meyer uses foreshadowing to clue her readers in to what will happen later in each novel and in the series as a whole. In *Twilight*, Bella reveals her greatest fear: that Edward will leave her. Even in the early moments of their relationship, Bella is "afraid that he might disappear in a sudden puff of smoke" and asks him to give her fair warning if he decides, as she puts it, "to ignore me for my own good." In the final chapter, "An Impasse," Bella is in the hospital recovering from James's attack, and Edward suggests that living hundreds of miles apart would be to her benefit. For Bella, even the thought of Edward being "someplace where [he] couldn't hurt [her] anymore" meant "pain that had nothing to do with broken bones, pain that was infinitely worse."

Edward's struggle to be or not to be with Bella is what he debates internally from the moment he meets her. As he explains to her in Carlisle's office, "I want you to be safe. And yet, I want to be with you. The two desires are impossible to reconcile. . . ." Realizing she attracts "accidents like a magnet," Edward asks her to be careful while he's on his brief hunting trip and again when he must put her in the care of Alice and Jasper in chapter 19, "Goodbyes," foreshadowing him making her promise not to be reckless before he disappears in *New Moon*. As evidence of how much he cares for her, Edward tells Bella that he would leave her: "if leaving is the right thing to do, then I'll hurt myself to keep from hurting you, to keep you safe." If Edward is happy with Bella, he feels he is later punished for dropping his guard and being careless. The guilt Edward feels for "exposing" her to James, especially after she is nearly killed, is enormous. That pattern repeats on Bella's 18th birthday. Edward also reveals in *Twilight* that he believes that Bella, as a human, would get over her feelings for him: "That's the beautiful thing about being human. . . . Things change." Even Bella's flirtation with danger in *New Moon* is hinted at in *Twilight*; the thought crosses her mind to "purposely put myself in danger to keep him close," as he has vowed to protect her. In *New Moon*, she follows through on that plan, keeping him present by conjuring his voice in her mind.

Foreshadowing takes other forms in the Twilight Saga, in Bella's instincts and dreams. In *New Moon*, after Jasper attacks Bella on her birthday, she feels Edward pulling away from her and has the premonition that things are about to get much worse. Her panic rises as Edward maintains his distance over the next few days at school, and she feels "like I was standing on an edge, a precipice somewhere much too high." That simile becomes a reality for Bella later in the novel, when she decides to cliff jump. Bella's dreams reflect her emotional state, but also allow her to process the craziness of her world, and are sometimes prophetic. In *Twilight*, after the day at La Push beach, Bella dreams that Jacob collapses onto the forest bed and is replaced by a red-brown

One of Stephenie's only complaints about her entire publishing experience concerns the cover for *New Moon* — unlike the apple, there's no special relevance to the tulip. "I was an active part of the covering process [for *Twilight*]. However, that experience is more the exception than the rule in the publishing world. . . . [Covers] are mostly up to the publisher and the marketing and sales departments. So I don't know what the tulip means — I didn't have anything to do with this one."

wolf, while Edward's skin glows in the sunlight. She revisits that same dream in *New Moon* after Jacob urges her to remember their conversation that day about Quileute legends, and her dream allows her to realize the truth: Jacob is a werewolf — a fact her subconscious mind knew ages before Jacob had turned. Earlier in *New Moon*, after spending the day with the Blacks and Clearwaters, Bella's recurring nightmare includes Sam Uley, whose presence is "unfriendly" and whose "shape seemed to shiver and change." Shortly thereafter, Bella begins to distrust Sam and blame him for what happens to Jake, before learning that Sam's shape shifts not just in her dreams but in reality. Bella's dreams are so vivid that she believes she is still dreaming when she awakes to find Edward with her in chapter 23, "The Truth." Bella is not alone in the world of literary characters who find themselves plagued with dreams both real and revealing. Nightmares blurring with reality plague the narrator Harker in Bram Stoker's *Dracula* and countless other characters in supernatural fiction as well as in literary classics like *Wuthering Heights*. Dreams are often used to reveal a character's fears and passions, allowing the narrative to explore what the character may not be able to see in waking life. Throughout human history, dreams have also been deeply connected to myths and legends as they are for Bella Swan.

Dreams merge with reality in *New Moon*, as do the Quileute legends that Jacob once thought were just scary stories. Jacob's fate, like Bella's, is inextricably tied to Edward's presence. Certain members of the Quileute nation turn into vampire-fighting wolves when the Cullens, or other "cold ones," inhabit the area. The real Quileute tribe lives in the area around the Quillayute River, in largest number in the reservation town of La Push, and has appeared in European histories since at least the 1700s. While their origin stories do not feature any vampiric creatures, there is a story about Dokibatt, the changer or transformer, who created the people from wolves. With this jumping-off point, Meyer adapted the actual legends to create the mythology in the Twilight Saga.

Just as Quileute legend helped shape Meyer's story so did Christian ideas about the afterlife and souls. It is Edward's firmly held belief that because he and his family are vampires, they are damned and soulless. For them, there will be no heaven — no matter how morally they live their lives on earth. This belief is what makes him so desperately reluctant to turn Bella into a vampire; he does not want to condemn her, to steal her soul. Bella, on the other hand, is not a religious person and therefore does not place the same value on losing her soul as Edward. To Bella, a soul is an abstract idea not a concrete fact. Losing Edward, not her soul, is the insufferable fate that she fears. But Carlisle makes her understand his son's vehemence: "If you believed as he did. Could you take away his soul?" Fortunately for Bella, the harrowing time Edward spends apart from her in *New Moon* slightly alters his beliefs about the afterlife. No longer hopeless, he reveals his openness to the possibility of heaven for the well-behaved vampire when Bella prevents him from exposing himself in the daylight of Volterra. He says, "Carlisle was right," and Bella understands what he means — vampires

can retain their souls and gain admission to heaven. Carlisle's ideas about the nature of eternity and souls mirror Mormon ideas about "eternal progressions." In Mormonism, it is believed that your actions in this life are carried with you into the next in "the immortality and eternal life of man," as God describes to Moses in the Latter-day Saints scripture. The Cullens, in their perfect beauty and high moral standing, are the epitome of this perfect eternal existence.

In *New Moon*, Bella finds herself not in heaven on earth but trapped in purgatory. Unlike vampires and werewolves, the change that takes over Bella and turns her into a "zombie" is all too real. Bella's depression may have a supernatural instigator, but the intensity of her pain and her way of dealing

"They're so intimate. You're right inside Bella's
mind – all her raw feelings and raw thoughts."
– Melissa Rosenberg on how the tone
of Stephenie's writing ties the book series together

with it — first by numbing herself to everything and everyone around her, then by engaging in self-destructive behavior — is an all-too-common phenomenon among young women. Bella's recurring nightmare of searching in the twilit forest until she realizes that there is "nothing but nothing" in her life now that Edward is gone indicates just how deeply she has been gutted by his departure. Feeling she can't talk to anyone about her relationship with Edward (not only because it's not her secret to share — she'd likely end up in the loony bin if she spoke about vampires as if they were real), Bella becomes even more withdrawn than she was when she first arrived in Forks, no longer communicating with her mother and hiding all of her thoughts and feelings. Her savior, her "earth-bound sun," is the warm-spirited and loving Jacob Black who she can't help but respond to honestly, openly, and with joy. Readers on Team Jacob point to how happy Bella is with him, how much more life-affirming he is than Edward. By the end of *New Moon* it seems like she has made her choice but *Eclipse* proves a decision between two such different suitors is one of the most difficult to make.

ROMEO AND JULIET
Though *Pride and Prejudice* helped to shape *Twilight*, *Romeo and Juliet* takes a much more central role in *New Moon*. Bella and Edward study it in English class, watch a film adaptation of it together, and discuss the actions of Romeo; Bella thinks of herself, Edward, and Jacob in terms of the play's characters; and Edward quotes Romeo when he sees Bella in Volterra. Stephenie Meyer also borrows plot points from William Shakespeare's play, with one lover leaving the other and a miscommunication about the heroine's death leading the hero to take his own life — but with Bella arriving in the nick of time to save Edward.

Since it was first published in 1597, *Romeo and Juliet* has captivated audiences with its story of star-crossed teenaged lovers, willing to give up their lives — their families, friends, and homes — for the other and unable to go on if the other is dead. Set in Verona, an Italian city about a three-hour drive from Volterra, the action of *Romeo and Juliet* begins with a street fight between the warring households of Capulets and Montagues. Just as the Quileutes and Cullens have an "ancient grudge" which breaks "to new mutiny" in *New Moon* with the Edward–Jacob rivalry, the fight between the families keeps Romeo and Juliet from going public with their love. Though Bella thinks of herself as Juliet and Edward as Romeo, there are also similarities between Bella and Romeo. Both keep their feelings to themselves, preferring to be their "own affections' counselor"

117

"I see a lot of aspects in Bella that I'd *like* to be able to be more of. And I think that's why most girls really love her too. She's an odd mix of things: she's got a very strong sense of self but she's entirely awkward and self-deprecating at the same time. And I think a lot of girls can relate to that. And she makes her decisions as most women do based pretty much solely on her gut instincts and doesn't get too wrapped up in – she gets very wrapped up in her own head but she follows her heart and just sort of ignores all the really conflicting feelings that she has. Bella really grows in *New Moon*. She becomes the woman that she ends up being in the rest of the series."

– Kristen Stewart

and become depressed in heartbreak, spend time alone, and vow not to forget their lost love. Romeo also has prophetic dreams; the night of the Capulet ball his "mind misgives / Some consequence yet hanging in the stars" that will lead to "untimely death." Like Bella with Edward, Romeo thinks of his love for Juliet in terms of dreams, and worries that it will vanish. Says Romeo, "I am afeard, / Being in night, all this is but a dream, / Too flatter-ing-sweet to be substantial."

Edward and Bella both think of the other as bringers of light, like Romeo does when he says of Juliet that "she doth teach the torches to burn bright!" Bella dreams of Edward sparkling in the sunshine the morning of her 18th birthday, and in her La Push dream she sees him glowing with light. When Edward describes the suffering he endured in Bella's absence at the end of *New Moon*, he compares his existence to "a moonless night." Now famously, Romeo equates Juliet with the sun in the balcony scene (Act II, scene ii); in *New Moon*, it is Bella who calls Jacob her sun, as he brings her back to life with his restora-tive light.

The threat of "love-devouring death" is ever constant in *Romeo and Juliet* as it is in the Twilight Saga. If Romeo were caught on the grounds of Capulet's estate, he would be killed; the intensity of his love for Juliet makes it worth risking his life. He would rather die knowing she returns his love than live without it: "My life were better ended by their hate / Than death proroguèd, wanting of thy love." For both couples, being apart is a fate worse than death. Spilled blood is the spark that sep-arates the lovers in both romances: it is Bella's blood at her birthday party which makes Edward leave, and it is Tybalt's blood shed by

Romeo's hand that brings about his banishment. After Mercutio and Tybalt are slain, Romeo must leave Verona or die. Like Edward's fate being decided by the Volturi, the royalty of the vampire world, Romeo's fate is decided by the Prince, the royalty of Verona. Juliet's plan to fake her death and escape to be with Romeo is analogous to Bella's; she needs to hear Edward's voice and goes cliff jumping, undertaking "a thing like death," not realizing that act (like Juliet's) will be mistaken for her actual death. Instead of a messenger being blocked by a quarantine town, Alice is unable to see that Bella lives because Jacob's presence blocks her vision. Playing the role of Balthazar, Rosalie is the bearer of bad news in *New Moon*, telling Edward that Bella has committed suicide. He vows to do the same, just as news of Juliet's death spurs Romeo to take his own life. For Romeo and Juliet, as for Bella and Edward, the only time suicide becomes a viable option is when their soul mate is dead. And in both stories, enemies threaten the lovers, in the form of Tybalt in *Romeo and Juliet*, and in the form of Victoria and the Volturi in *New Moon*.

For the epigraph of *New Moon*, Stephenie Meyer selected part of Friar Lawrence's speech before he weds Romeo and Juliet: "These violent delights have violent ends / And in their triumph die, like fire and powder, / Which, as they kiss, consume." His speech concludes with advice to "love moderately," something Romeo, Juliet, Edward, and Bella all seem incapable of. Though Juliet changes her mind upon falling in love with Romeo, Bella's opinion of marriage can be well summed up with Juliet's pithy line on the subject from the first act of the play: "It is an honor that I dream not of." At the end of *New Moon*, it is an "honor" that Bella has to consider seriously if she wants

> *". . . love gave someone the power*
> *to break you."*
>
> *Bella (New Moon, 219)*

Edward to be the one to turn her into a vampire. On Stephenie Meyer's website, she revealed that she was originally thinking of using part of Juliet's speech from Act III, scene ii (where she awaits Romeo on her wedding night) as the epigraph for *New Moon* — "Come, gentle night; come, loving, black-browed night; / Give me my Romeo; and, when I shall die, / Take him and cut him out in little stars, / And he will make the face of heaven so fine / That all the world will be in love with night" — but Stephenie opted to go with "the warning" over the "romance."

Like Edward sneaking into Bella's room without Charlie's knowledge, Romeo and Juliet consummate their marriage in the Capulet home, while her father is betrothing her to Paris. Capulet favors Paris just as Charlie favors Jacob over Edward and, viewed from the fathers' perspectives, those matches would bring the most happiness to their daughters. Capulet worries about how upset Juliet is by Tybalt's death and hurries her marriage to Paris. Paris explains to Friar Lawrence, "her father counts it dangerous / That she do give her sorrow so much sway, / And in his wisdom hastes our marriage / To stop the inundation of her tears." Imagine if Capulet had to deal with the months of depression that Charlie bore witness to as Bella mourned Edward. As Bella develops stronger feelings for Jacob, she compares him to Paris, wondering what *Romeo and Juliet* would be like if Paris's character were more than a sketch of suitor, if he were an actual person who brought joy to Juliet's life after Romeo left her. Like Edward thanking Jacob for taking care of Bella in his absence, Romeo feels sympathy for Paris because of their shared love for Juliet; they share a kinship, but that does not stop Romeo from killing Paris because he stands in his way of Juliet's tomb.

In Stephenie Meyer's retelling of *Romeo and Juliet* with Edward and Bella, there is much less bloodshed in the final act. Bella arrives in time to save Edward, letting him know that she's very much alive. But inasmuch as the story ends with the star-crossed lovers reunited and reassured of their love for each other, Bella and Edward still have to face the Volturi, Victoria, the consequences if they break the treaty, Charlie's ire, and the feelings Bella has developed for Jacob. Like *Romeo and Juliet*, *New Moon* ends with a "glooming peace."

chapter 13

Adapting
New Moon

Chris Weitz wrote an open letter to fans after he was hired to direct *New Moon* to ease their worries about Catherine Hardwicke being replaced.

Melissa Rosenberg started in on the script for *New Moon* while *Twilight* was still in post-production in an effort to give herself a little more time than she'd had for the first script in the series. (And she went straight on to *Eclipse* once the *New Moon* script was finished.) "It's really been five days a week on *Dexter* and two days a week on one of the Twilight movies for about two and a half years now," said Rosenberg around the time that production on *New Moon* wrapped. After developing their working relationship on *Twilight*, Rosenberg sought out Stephenie Meyer's help a lot more often for *New Moon*. "She has a very detailed mythology, very, very intricate," says Rosenberg, "and not all of it's on the page . . . I want to make sure not to violate that but also to glean some ideas from her." Of course, the bulk of *New Moon* is spent following Bella as she handles her breakup with Edward, which worried Robert Pattinson fans — would he only be in a few scenes at the beginning and end of the film? Said Rosenberg, "The challenge of *New Moon* is that Edward, our romantic lead, disappears — although it's

"He had the confidence before [he put on the muscle].
It was so clear that he was right."

– Kristen Stewart on Taylor Lautner as Jacob Black

interesting in the book he doesn't really disappear. He physically disappears but he is very present in Bella's mind and so that was really what we were working off of — keeping him alive in the way that Stephenie does in the book." The solution was to change the Edward voice Bella hears into an apparition that she — and the audience — can both see and hear.

More controversial than Edward's physical absence from the action was the question of who would be directing the sequel. Discussions of *New Moon* during the *Twilight* pre-release press tour suggested that Catherine Hardwicke would return, but by the time the cast and Catherine were in Paris it was announced that she would not be directing the sequel. The official reason was a scheduling conflict; Hardwicke requested more time for pre-production than Summit was willing to allow. In a statement, Summit said their projected release date "does not work with Ms. Hardwicke's required prep time to bring her vision of the film to the big screen." The Twilight Saga films were moving forward at vampire speed with production on *Eclipse* to follow as soon as possible after *New Moon*. The newcomer at the helm was Chris Weitz who had, with his brother Paul, directed and produced 1999's *American Pie* as well as adapted and directed 2002's *About a Boy* from the novel by Nick Hornby. The brothers along with co-writer Peter Hedges were nominated for an Academy Award for that screenplay. His second adaptation of a beloved novel, Philip Pullman's *The Golden Compass*, was less well received. Though it's gone on to earn an impressive box office (particularly in international markets), the 2007 film was plagued with differences between the studio and the creative team. *The Golden Compass* featured a wealth of CG animals, playing the daemons to the humans, and that experience helped Weitz when it came time to put the wolf pack on screen.

But, first things first, Chris Weitz had to read *New Moon*, which he did non-stop over the course of a day and a half at a retreat in California, which had a sweat lodge. Revealed Weitz, "Actually, my only pause was for a sweat lodge during which I asked the Quileute ancestors to come and give me good luck. Somewhere Jacob Black was pleased. I was channeling Team Jacob because he needs it in this movie. Everyone already knows about Edward."

Team Taylor also needed some support as the actor worked hard to prove to Summit Entertainment that he should keep his role as Jacob Black in the sequel. Famously putting on the muscle weight, Taylor Lautner landed the gig and had the support of his cast mates, director, and the public as the production team — some returning from the first film, some new faces — assembled in Vancouver, British Columbia, to film *New Moon*.

chapter 14

Descendents
of the Wolf

ALEX MERAZ
AS PAUL

❀ ❀ ❀

Playing hot-headed Quileute werewolf Paul is Alex Meraz, born January 10, 1985. The Arizonian was uniquely qualified for the role, having not only the required Native American descent (he is a member of the Purépecha nation), but also serious dance and fight training. Meraz has won several Capoeira tournaments (a Brazilian form of martial arts fused with dance), and is accomplished in both breakdancing and traditional indigenous danc-

ing. Though he is perfectly suited for the role, it was the encouragement of his wife, Kim, who is a big fan of the novels, that really pushed him to audition. Before *New Moon*, he appeared in the Pocahontas-inspired feature film *The New World* (2005); *Dancing with Spirit*, a six-part Bravo showcase of Native American dance that allowed him to showcase his skills; and historical television specials *We Shall Remain* and *The American Experience*. One of the things Meraz appreciates about the Twilight movies is the opportunity to play a Native American outside of the "leather and feather" stereotype, as co-star Chaske Spencer calls it. Meraz enthused, "I think it's time for us to kind of rewrite what Hollywood's take on Native Americans was, which was long hair blowing, noble kind of people. . . . So now you see something in a contemporary setting, and you see us to be humans. It's great."

CHASKE SPENCER
AS SAM ULEY

❀ ❀ ❀

Quileute wolf pack leader Sam Uley is played by Idaho-born Chaske (pronounced Chess-kay) Spencer, who has Lakota Sioux heritage. Chaske attended Lewis Clark State College for a year, before buying a one-way ticket to New York City to pursue acting work. After living like a stereotypical starving artist for a while, bartending and catering, his big break came with the 2002 film *Skins* (opposite *New Moon*'s Graham Greene). After *Skins*, Chaske performed in about one project a year, TV movie *DreamKeeper* in 2003, video game *Red Dead Revolver* in 2004, and miniseries *Into the West* in 2005. Then came *New Moon*. The actor auditioned for all the wolf pack roles, but the casting directors must have seen the alpha male in him. As soon as he got the role, Chaske read *New Moon* and *Eclipse*. He told *Vanity Fair*, "I really tried to relate to those characters, do my job . . . and then go to the gym." And though he was in shape before filming, his transformation was as extreme as his pack-mates'. He admits, "One day, I stepped out of the shower, took a look at myself, and I didn't recognize my own body." So far, all of Chaske's roles have been Native American–specific, but *New Moon* has opened up a wider variety of parts

to him. He knows his career has phased into an entirely different beast: "It's a milestone. It's changed our lives."

TYSON HOUSEMAN
AS QUIL ATEARA

❀ ❀ ❀

Considering 70,000 men auditioned for five wolf pack spots, it's pretty amazing that Tyson Houseman just seemed to stumble into one of them. The Edmonton native of Cree descent had a friend show him a casting call on Craigslist, and he thought it was worth a try. "I had never been to an audition before in my life but I said I'll go try it out," recalls Tyson. He had just graduated from Edmonton's Victoria School of the Arts the previous year, and had moved to Vancouver. Tyson explained, "I wasn't sure if I wanted to go to university. Acting wasn't on the very top of my list that I wanted to pursue in life, but since I got this part things started happening so fast." Jacob's goofball friend Quil Ateara was his first role, but with that kind of debut on the international film scene, it won't be his last.

KIOWA GORDON
AS EMBRY CALL

❀ ❀ ❀

All of the *Twilight* stars can say Stephenie Meyer changed their lives, but Kiowa Gordon benefited from her direct influence. Meyer attends the same ward of the Church of Jesus Christ of Latter-day Saints as Kiowa's mother, and espying the young Hualapai there, Meyer recommended he audition for the role. His

Chaske Spencer and Tinsel Korey attend the screening of *New Moon* at the 6th Annual Red Nation Film Festival.

tribe is from northern Arizona, and while he spent part of his childhood on a reservation, he now calls Cave Creek, Arizona, home (along with fellow shapeshifter Alex Meraz). Though Kiowa got a C in his acting class at Cactus Shadows High School, that didn't stop him from landing the role of Embry Call, one of Jacob's best friends. He says, "I knew this was something I had to be a part of. I would have been crazy to pass this movie up." *New Moon* opened up new roles for him: he stars in horror flick *Into the Darkness* and thriller *Murder for Dummys*.

BRONSON PELLETIER AS JARED

❋ ❋ ❋

Completing the wolf pack as Jared is Bronson Pelletier, a Canadian actor of Cree and Métis descent born on the last day of 1986. Before *New Moon*, Bronson was best known for his roles on the children's programs *Dinosapien* and the Aboriginal teen drama *renegadepress.com*. The Vancouver resident is known among the other "wolves" as a jokester, and he tried to bring the same tone to his role as Jared. Like the rest of the pack actors, Bronson raves about their camaraderie while filming. He explained that the chemistry on set was "organic and natural; it's real. We're not putting on a charade. I plan on knowing these guys for the rest of my life." Pelletier realizes that the wolf pack doesn't get a lot of screen time, but he's determined to make the most of it. "There's no such thing as a small role," says the young actor. "I bring it all to the table and see what happens."

Kiowa Gordon, Christian Serratos, Edi Gathegi, Chaske Spencer, Bronson Pelletier, and Alex Meraz meet fans on November 5, 2009.

TINSEL KOREY
AS EMILY YOUNG

❊ ❊ ❊

Playing "the wolf girl" Emily, Sam Uley's sweet but scarred partner, is Tinsel Korey, a Canadian actress of Anishinabe descent. Tinsel's Native status was a subject of controversy for the adopted child, who suffered allegations that she had falsified her heritage. Regardless of her genetics, Tinsel has found success in television shows such as *Da Vinci's* *Inquest*, *Godiva's*, *Rabbit Fall*, and *The Guard*, numerous TV movies, and the Spielberg mini-series *Into the West*. Tinsel's film credits include *Unnatural & Accidental* (2006) and indie sleeper success *Mothers & Daughters* (2008). The multi-talented actress is also a painter and musician, who performed at the 2008 Aboriginal Achievement Awards and is currently at work on her first album. She'll also appear in psychological thriller *Stained* in 2010. After breaking into the acting business in 2004, Korey is finally seeing her dedication pay off: "I know this is the pinnacle of where things are about to change for me. . . . It was happening gradually but I just have an internal feeling that it's about to get a little crazy."

GRAHAM GREENE
AS HARRY CLEARWATER

✦ ✦ ✦

A veteran actor with stage experience and over 100 film and television credits to his name, Graham Greene is one of the leading Native actors in North America. Unlike others in the movie business, Graham didn't grow up wanting to be an actor — he worked in construction and then in the music industry. But when a friend coerced him into acting in his play, more work followed. Since his film debut in 1983, Graham has starred in small Canadian films he would never see in theaters alongside his Hollywood blockbusters such as *Die Hard: With a Vengeance* (1995), *The Green Mile* (1999), and most notably, the Kevin Costner epic *Dances with Wolves* (1990). Graham's role as Sioux medicine man Kicking Bird earned him an Academy Award nomination. The celebrated actor has also appeared on television shows ranging from *Murder, She Wrote* to the hit Canadian comedy *The Red Green Show*. He joined the Twilight Saga in *New Moon* to play Harry Clearwater, a friend of Charlie, a Quileute elder, and the maker of the best fish-fry in Washington. Despite his tremendous success over a two-decade career, Graham has practical advice for aspiring actors: "First, get your cab driver's license. Then learn to wait tables and how to tend bar."

GIL BIRMINGHAM
AS BILLY BLACK

✦ ✦ ✦

It's well known that all the wolf-pack boys had to pump it up for their roles, but it's much less well known that Gil Birmingham, who plays the wheelchair-bound Billy Black, could have out-benched them all in his bodybuilding heyday. The actor's first break was actually a guest spot in Diana Ross's "Muscles" video, followed by a stint as Conan the Barbarian at Universal Studios Hollywood. After his 1986 television debut on *Riptide*, he landed numerous TV guest spots, appearing on shows such as *Buffy the Vampire Slayer*, *Body & Soul*, *Charmed*, *Veronica Mars*, and *Nip/Tuck*, as well as the *Into the West* miniseries (along with Chaske Spencer, Tinsel Korey, and Graham Greene). His film roles include the award-winning drama *The Doe Boy* and the Ben Stiller comedy *Night at the Museum*. Like many of his Twilight co-stars, Gil is also a musician, and has been playing the guitar since age 10.

chapter 15

The Volturi

DAKOTA FANNING
AS JANE

❀ ❀ ❀

With her breakthrough role as the daughter of a mentally handicapped man in *I Am Sam*, Hannah Dakota Fanning broke the hearts of international audiences when she was merely six years old. Born February 23, 1994, Fanning's had remarkable success in both television and film. On the small screen, she's played young versions of both Ellen DeGeneres and Calista Flockhart; she's done voice-over work; she's appeared on numerous primetime TV shows such as *ER*, *CSI*, *Friends*, *Family Guy*; and starred in the Steven Spielberg sci-fi miniseries *Taken*. On the big screen she's done major blockbusters like *War of the Worlds* (opposite Tom Cruise), children's classics *The Cat in the Hat* (2003) and *Charlotte's Web* (2006), independent films such as the controversial *Hounddog* (2007) and short film *Cutlass* (with Kristen Stewart), and recorded voice-over work for the title role in the highly regarded 3D adaptation *Coraline* (2009). In 2006, at age 12, she was the youngest person to ever be inducted into the Academy of Motion Picture Arts and Sciences. The accomplished actress was excited to be cast as Jane, the telepathic torturer, in *New Moon*: "It's kind of evil, something I've never done before, and it's a vampire. . . . It's really cool." Co-star Michael Sheen found Fanning's to be the most disturbing transformation of all, tweeting that she looked like "an evil Red Riding Hood." And *New Moon* director Chris Weitz was pleased that even in a dramatically different role, Dakota lived up to her reputation: "what you expect from Dakota Fanning is uncannily grown-up, experienced, and clever acting — and that's what she did." Despite all her success, Dakota hasn't been misled by fame, and attends a regular school, is a cheerleader, a Girl Scout, and an avid reader and knitter. Her post–Twilight Saga projects include a reunion with Kristen Stewart in *The Runaways*.

MICHAEL SHEEN
AS ARO

❋ ❋ ❋

Before his management ever mentioned the part of Volturi leader Aro in *New Moon*, Welsh actor Michael Sheen had the books on his radar: they were a favorite of his daughter Lily. Born February 5, 1969, Michael Sheen attended London's Royal Academy of Dramatic Art and started his career with acclaimed stage performances in *Frost/Nixon* and *Amadeus*. He transitioned to TV and film in 1993, and was cast in major roles such as the werewolf leader Lucian in the Underworld trilogy, British Prime Minister Tony Blair in *The Queen*, reporter David Frost in *Frost/Nixon*, and soccer manager Brian Clough in *The Damned United*. Commenting

At the Rome Film Festival, Charlie Bewley (Demetri), Melissa Rosenberg, Cameron Bright, and Jamie Campbell Bower arrive on the red carpet.

on his successful career, Sheen noticed one similarity in his otherwise diverse roles: "It's interesting that in searching for monsters to play, you often end up playing leaders."

JAMIE CAMPBELL BOWER AS CAIUS

❀ ❀ ❀

Jamie Campbell Bower was still in boarding school when he got his big break: at age 17 he was cast in the 2007 Tim Burton dark musical *Sweeney Todd: The Demon Barber of Fleet Street* opposite acting heavyweights Johnny Depp and Helena Bonham Carter. He was overcome when he got the news: "I think I wee'd myself," he told the *New York Observer*. Born November 22, 1988, the London-born Bower was heavily involved in musical theater while boarding at Bedales School in the countryside. He thought he wanted to be a West-End theater actor until *Sweeney Todd*. One semester short of graduation, he continued to pursue roles in film and television, landing Caius in *New Moon*, and a role on AMC miniseries *The Prisoner*, opposite Ian McKellen. He's also jumped aboard another wildly successful franchise, and will be appearing in the final installment of the Harry Potter series as Gellert Grindelwald, an old friend of Dumbledore.

Also appearing in Guy Ritchie's *RocknRolla* and Dutch film *Winter in Wartime*, Jamie is an avid Twitterer, keeping his growing fan base apprised of his daily adventures and signing each post with an "X" kiss.

CAMERON BRIGHT AS ALEC

❀ ❀ ❀

When Cameron Bright (born Cameron Douglas Crigger on January 26, 1993) found out he'd been cast in *New Moon*, his guy friends dismissed it, saying, "It's a chick movie." But Bright feels differently, "It was really good. I'm glad to be a part of it." Victoria, British Columbia–born Bright came to *New Moon* having already established his acting chops: he gained instant notoriety for his role as a 10-year-old who tells a widow (Nicole Kidman) that he's her dead husband in *Birth*, and has appeared in big-ticket feature films such as *The Butterfly Effect, X-Men: The Last Stand, Thank You for Smoking, Ultraviolet,* and *Juno*. And while his profile has risen from his role as the sense-blocking Volturi Alec, he's less worried about the throngs of fans at events than female friends who pester him with one essential question: "Can you get me Robert Pattinson's autograph?"

CHRISTOPHER HEYERDAHL AS MARCUS

❀ ❀ ❀

Though countless actors would die to join the ranks of the undead royalty, Christopher Heyerdahl had immortality offered to him on a silver platter. The Canadian actor didn't even audition for the part of Marcus, the calm and rational member of the Volturi who can read people's emotions. His agent simply called and

offered him the role. "I guess they figured my bizarre kind of face would be perfect for a guy who's been dead over 3,000 years," jokes the actor. With a career spanning over 20 years, Heyerdahl has plenty of experience playing supernatural beings. He's bared his fangs twice already, on *The Hunger* and as classic vamp Nosferatu on *Are You Afraid of the Dark?*, played a Wraith on *Stargate: Atlantis*, a torturer from hell on *Supernatural*, and even "Bigfoot" on *Sanctuary*. Add in projects like Stephen King's *The Dead Zone*, *Andromeda*, *Stargate: SG-1*, and films like *Bleeders* (1997), *Blade: Trinity* (2004), and *The Chronicles of Riddick* (2004) and Heyerdahl easily has more experience with the paranormal than any of the other Twilight Saga cast members. The actor has also appeared in a number of French films, in which he performs *en français*.

In an interview with the Twilight Lexicon, Heyerdahl explained his approach to portraying Marcus: "Does he always believe the decisions his fellows are making — the rest of the triumvirate — does he believe in the choices they're making? Not always. But he believes in the Volturi and that, I think, is the fun thing for me to play with Marcus is to not always agree."

chapter 16

Shooting the Moon

Filming *New Moon* presented a whole new set of challenges. Taylor Lautner had risen from supporting cast to a serious love interest, and had a lot more screen time. He had to make Jacob's mid-film transformation from nice guy to snarling wolf credible. Taylor explained, "He's a lot different than he was before. He transforms mid-story — in the first half, he's *Twilight* Jacob. I'm wearing a wig. My character's very clumsy, outgoing, and friendly. When he transforms into a werewolf, he becomes something very different. It's like I'm playing a split personality. Which is tricky, because sometimes I've had to play pre- and post-transformation Jacob on the same day." Chris Weitz encouraged Taylor to explore Jacob's darker side, saying, "It was a question of letting him hit his range, which included

being angry, resentful, dangerous, and violent." And of course there was the matter of spending all that time shirtless and freezing in the pouring rain. Taylor might have looked hot, but he certainly wasn't feeling the heat. "I was freezing in those little shorts. I just had

was finished, his co-stars had complete confidence in him. "He devoted himself to that transformation for a year. But it's not even about how he looks — though he's gorgeous and shirtless and sexy for most of the film. He's just so, so good as Jacob. And he can handle the pressure," says Nikki Reed. "I know it. Taylor's going to steal the show." Kristen felt the same way. Though she quipped to *Entertainment Weekly*, "We objectify the boys in this movie and I am down with that," it was clear that Kristen saw past the wolf-pack six-pack to Taylor's stand-out performance.

While Bella undergoes no physical transformation, save aging one year, Kristen had a complex emotional arc to portray in *New Moon*. "The difficult part was feeling emotions that are set in an unreality," explained Kristen, "feeling emotions that you're told, 'You couldn't ever feel this. You could never feel as gutted by a boyfriend as she could be by this vampire.' So I was always kind of feeling like I wasn't doing enough, but I feel like that with every movie I do so . . ."

The scenes of Bella wandering in the woods, at first screaming for Edward and then wandering aimlessly until she trips and collapses on the forest bed, were filmed on location at night. The reality of the setting and the exhaustion that kicks in as a long night shoot drags on aided Kristen's performance. In an interview with ChucktheMovieGuy.com, Kristen explained, "I think that it actually helped that we shot all night. I was by myself in the woods wandering around. It felt real. . . . You can conceptualize everything [about your performance], you know, to such a ridiculous degree but when you walk on set and have to

to take myself into another world so that during the scene I wasn't shivering." On the Jacob–Bella dynamic that grows over the course of *New Moon*, Taylor said, "It was easy with Kristen, easy to bring that relationship alive, with the help of Chris."

But after all the challenges he had in becoming the new Jacob Black, when the film

Kristen Stewart and Anna Kendrick rehearse the scene where Bella and Jessica leave the movie theater after seeing zombie flick *The Dead Come Back*.

live it, you can't actually be thinking about all of these, like, metaphorical ideas behind why this story makes sense to you in your life and whatever. It's about, like, breathing it. . . . The only reason I was able to do that on this [film] as comfortably as I feel I did was because of Chris [Weitz], 'cause he made me feel really safe."

From scenes shot all alone in the dark woods to those with hundreds of extras in sunny Montepulciano, Italy, *New Moon* was a

challenging and varied shoot for its lead actress. The citizens of Volterra dressed in red robes were, in great numbers, Twilight fans who got to appear as extras. Shooting the scene where Bella races across the square to push Edward out of the sunlight, Kristen found the audience of extras a surprisingly awesome addition. As she and Rob finished the take, there was "instantly an eruption of applause and people so like [draws breath in], like screaming. And it was like doing theater and I've never done that and it was a different experience but, like, the energy being thrown at you . . . I think that made the scene better." One scene that Kristen just had to grin and bear was the cliff-jumping scene or, more specifically, the drowning part. The scene was filmed in a massive water tank that was churned by a wave generator; the cliff was added in digitally to the background in post-production. "Kristen was a trooper," reported producer Wyck Godfrey. "She *hates* the water . . . if you don't like the water and you have these huge waves coming at you — the terror is real. It really wasn't fun for her, and she was sick when we shot it."

Not only was there a new director at the helm of the sequel but also a whole new filming location. Instead of returning to the Portland area, it made more fiscal sense to shoot in British Columbia, Canada. That meant that scenes at the Swan or Cullen houses, at the high school, or any other location seen in *Twilight* would have to be matched as closely as possible with new locations in Vancouver. "It was really nerve-racking," said Chris Weitz, "because I thought people would notice and be upset; it was a puzzle to get it

For the movie theater scenes, the *New Moon* crew shot at the Paramount Theatre (opposite) for the exterior shots and the Ridge Theatre (above) for the interiors.

just right. The outside of the school is all CGI, we built the stairway for the school and took stills. In the Cullens' house I also tried to show different rooms in the house to add to the feeling of the house." Finding locations to stand in for La Push was not too difficult on the rugged B.C. coast. While filming near Tofino, producer Bill Bannerman said, "The weather is perfect for us: rainy, dismal, in the sense of the visuals, the mist on the ocean, the cloudiness, the erratic wind activity. Everything is exactly what it should be. . . . You have to feel, which is perceived quite in detail, quite a bit in detail in the book, the Forks and La Push area. It forces you, when you put it to a visual medium, to go into really remote locations to try to find that texture. And so this is one element we couldn't find anywhere else. That's why we love it [here]."

But some locations proved impossible to find and the cliff that Bella jumps off had to be created from a composite of shots and CGI. *New Moon* featured a lot more computer-generated imagery than *Twilight*: the wolves, of course, as well as smaller details like Kristen's eye color in certain scenes (where the pouring rain or pounding water made it impossible for her to keep her eyes open and Bella-brown contacts in) and the transitions in the "time passes" sequence. Instead of having

Lost in Translation: In the kitchen, Jacob says to Bella, *"Kwop kilawtley,"* which means "stay with me forever" in Quileute. Close readers of *New Moon* will remember that *"la tua cantante"* means "your singer"; Bella's blood sings for Edward and Aro knows it.

fILMING LOCATIONS

With *New Moon*, the Twilight Tourism Effect spread from Forks, WA, and the Portland, OR, area to Vancouver, BC, and all the way to *bella Italia*.

The Cullen house: Finding a house that matched the aesthetic of the Portland "Nike House" was the challenge for *New Moon*'s location manager. At 118 Stevens Drive in West Vancouver, the production found the vampires' new home, designed by award-winning architect Arthur Erickson.

The rescue scene: Long Beach (located near Wickaninnish Beach) in the Pacific Rim National Park Reserve was the setting for Jacob's rescue of drowning Bella.

Forks High School: The set designers took Vancouver's David Thompson Secondary School (East 55th Avenue) and made it look as close as possible to *Twilight*'s Forks High, adding flags along the window of the cafeteria, round tables, and blue support beams as well as Forks Spartans swag. The rest was done in post-production.

Movie theater: The scenes of Bella, Jacob, and Mike inside the movie theater were shot at Ridge Theatre (3131 Arbutus Street) while the exterior for both that movie night and Bella and Jessica's were filmed at Paramount Theatre at 652 Columbia Street in New Westminster.

Volterra: Though Volterra is a real-life Tuscan town, the *New Moon* crew filmed in Montepulciano (pictured opposite), also the location for scenes in *Gladiator* and *The English Patient*. Many locations were used: Vicolo della Concordia, Piazza delle Erbe, Piazza Grande, Piazza San Francesco (where Bella races across the square), and the hallway of the Town Hall (where Edward and Bella reunite).

---

the screen blank and the words "October . . . November . . . December . . . January" appear in a direct imitation of the novel, Melissa Rosenberg came up with the idea of having the seasons change outside Bella's bedroom window. The seamless passing time scene was created using CGI. Weitz revealed that "the windows were covered by green screen. We used a robotic camera for revolvement to mimic the original hand camera as much as possible. I'm not sure if you noticed but with each revolvement the room changes, there are less pictures of her friends and the room gets more sparse." As with the first film, Little, Brown released *The Twilight Saga New Moon: The Complete Illustrated Movie Companion* written by Mark Cotta Vaz, which details the shooting experience.

While Taylor and Kristen had an undeniably more intensive shoot on *New Moon* than

on *Twilight*, Robert Pattinson had more room to make the most of his limited but crucial Edward scenes. Asked about filming his slow-motion walk across the Forks High parking lot, Robert laughed, "It's the hardest and most humiliating experience in the world. . . . And it was a long walk, like 40 or 50 feet, and there's nothing to it except trying to look sultry or whatever." With Kristen laughing off-camera, he managed to get a few takes in where he "didn't look like he had a limp." Sultry walks aside, it was a relatively easy shoot for Robert Pattinson. Not only was Taylor bearing most of the heartthrob weight but *New Moon* is his "favorite of the books. I understood everything about it, well not everything, but I had a really specific idea of how I wanted to play it, which influenced how I played the first one and the

Kristen Stewart and Taylor Lautner at the November 16, 2009, premiere of *New Moon*, which happened to be the night of an actual new moon.

SONG BY SCENE
THE NEW MOON SOUNDTRACK

1. "Meet Me on the Equinox," Death Cab for Cutie

   The lead single for the soundtrack plays over the film's end credits.

2. "Friends," Band of Skulls

   After seeing a vision of Edward, Bella takes a ride on a stranger's motorcycle.

3. "Hearing Damage," Thom Yorke

   Charlie and Harry hunt the wolves; the wolf pack chases Victoria through the woods; Bella climbs up the cliff.

4. "Possibility," Lykke Li

   Bella mourns Edward, staring out her bedroom window as months pass.

5. "A White Demon Love Song," The Killers

   End credits.

6. "Satellite Heart," Anya Marina

   After Jasper's attack, Edward drives Bella home in her truck. It may be the first song they listen to on her new Emmett-installed stereo.

7. "I Belong to You (New Moon Remix)," Muse

   Jessica and Bella have their not-so-successful girls' night out.

8. "Rosyln," Bon Iver & St. Vincent

   The day after Bella's birthday, Edward doesn't show up for school, but is waiting for Bella when she arrives home.

9. "Done All Wrong," Black Rebel Motorcycle Club

   Vampire Girl meets Wolf Girl when the pack brings Bella to Emily's house.

10. "Monsters," Hurricane Bells

    Bella drives to school on her birthday and Edward walks across the parking lot . . . in slow motion.

11. "The Violet Hour," Sea Wolf

    Alice throws Bella a birthday party at the Cullens'.

12. "Shooting the Moon," OK Go

    Motorcycle montage: Jacob rebuilds the bikes with Bella at his side.

13. "Slow Life," Grizzly Bear with Victoria Legrand

    As Bella drowns, she is reunited with Edward in her mind's eye.

14. "No Sound But the Wind," Editors

    After the vote at the Cullens', Edward and Bella drive back to her house before meeting Jacob on the road.

15. "New Moon (The Meadow)," Alexandre Desplat

    End credits.

    (Bonus) "All I Believe In," The Magic Numbers & Amadou & Mariam

    Bella turns this song off as she and Jake work on the motorcycle rebuild.

    (Bonus) "Solar Midnite," Lupe Fiasco

    The soundtrack to the movie-within-the-movie Face Punch.

    (Bonus) "Die Fledermaus – Duettino: Ach, Ich Darf Nicht Hin Zu Dir," (Strauss) APM Orchestra

    Volturi–style elevator music.

> "I can't imagine anyone else playing Bella. I think Kristen is a fantastic actress. I've never seen anyone work harder and just beat themselves up to give the most authentic experience in each scene."
>
> – producer Wyck Godfrey

third one." Watching *Twilight* and responding to the fans' reactions to it, Robert knew what he wanted to "fix" about his performance: "It's an older performance, I think; I had much more control over the aesthetic of the character." Said Robert before the film's release, "They're saying that it's testing really well, the movie, and I just think that after the Comic-Con where you can just literally put the word 'Twilight' on the screen and people will start screaming. I mean, you could just do that; that's a good enough test."

Rob's Comic-Con market test proved to be good enough. On November 20, 2009, *New Moon* opened in 4,024 theaters across America and beat the box-office record for best opening day, previously held by *The Dark Knight*. The tickets kept selling and *New Moon* was hugely successful for Summit Entertainment and the franchise. The cast was everywhere: being interviewed for print, TV, and online media; touring the world to promote the film; and their likenesses were plastered on *New Moon* merchandise everywhere from Hot Topic to Burger King. Film critics, as with *Twilight*, were for the most part tepid in their response, with *The Guardian* calling the franchise "a little anaemic" but praising Kristen's development

as an actor and *The Hollywood Reporter* naming Chris Weitz a "smart choice for the material." Whether they were returning to the theater time and again or slagging it with internet spoofs, everyone was talking about *New Moon* and its stars. Though it hardly seemed possible, the Twilight Saga was only growing in popularity, and anticipation for *The Twilight Saga: Eclipse* was even higher than for *New Moon*. Luckily, Summit Entertainment had Alice's foresight with the franchise, and slated *Eclipse* for a June 30, 2010, release.

THE SOUNDTRACK

As soon as the *New Moon* script was finalized, work began on putting together a track listing that could match the caliber of songs on the first movie's soundtrack. In an interview with Spin.com, Alex Patsavas explained her approach to *New Moon*: "There's a lot of separation and longing and loss in the movie; the bands and lyrics and sound and arrangements had to reflect that. Some folks, like Lykke Li, the Killers, Grizzly Bear, OK Go, and Anya Marina, all came into the cutting room and sat with Chris to watch the movie and talk about their contributions. Other tracks were submitted with the movie in mind. I think it's very difficult to succeed without any context." For the lead single, Patsavas worked again with a band she had years earlier while music-supervising *The O.C.*: Washington's Death Cab for Cutie. Death Cab's bassist Nick Harmer said, "It just seemed a perfect synergy that a band from the Northwest would create a song for a series of novels set in the Northwest. We wrote 'Meet Me at the Equinox' to reflect the celestial themes and motifs that run through-out the Twilight series and we wanted to capture that desperate feeling of endings and beginnings that so strongly affect the main characters."

The soundtrack was supposed to come out on October 20, 2009, but due to the "over-whelming and unprecedented" demand, fans got their hands on it four days early. The Chop Shop album debuted at number two on the Billboard Top 200 before climbing to number one the next week. Shortly thereafter it was certified platinum.

For the score, Chris Weitz hired Alexandre Desplat, with whom he had worked on *The Golden Compass*. The French composer has twice been nominated for an Academy Award for his film scores (*The Queen, The Curious Case of Benjamin Button*). Replacing Carter Burwell, Desplat decided not to listen to the *Twilight* score. As he said to Examiner.com, "No, not only did I not listen to it, but I didn't even watch the movie. I didn't want to be influenced by it. Carter is a great composer and I loved his scores for the Coen Brothers. And I knew that if I went there, I would be in danger, because I knew that I would enjoy it and then be influenced by it." Working with Weitz (who speaks French), they decided their only musical reference would be another French film composer, Maurice Jarre (*Lawrence of Arabia, Doctor Zhivago, A Passage to India*). The score was also released on October 16.

Fire and Ice

In *Twilight*, Bella Swan decides she wants to become a vampire; from her point of view, it's the only way for her and Edward to be together. In *New Moon*, she loses the future that she had imagined and hoped for herself — an eternity with Edward — and then has it promised back to her. In *Eclipse*, Bella realizes just how high a price she will have to pay for an eternity spent as a Cullen. As Bella inches toward her high school graduation — the usual time a teenager is first granted true freedom from the rules of her parents and the structure of school — she battles with the strictures placed on her by Charlie, by Edward, and those made necessary by being privy to a world where monsters roam among unknowing humans.

At 18 years old, Bella may legally be an adult, but she is still restricted like a child: she is grounded by Charlie for taking off to Italy in *New Moon*; Edward prevents her from seeing Jacob, disabling her truck and having Alice "kidnap" her; she can't confide in any of her human friends, or in her mother, because of the nature of her secrets; she and Edward cannot get much more physical than a bit of kissing or else he may lose control and hurt her; and, once the mysterious vampires make their presence known, Bella is "babysat" by protectors — sometimes even by those younger than her, like Jacob or Seth. Jacob jokes with Bella about "controlling, abusive teenage relationships," pointing out that she feels she has to ask Edward's permission to visit La Push. Edward also realizes his behavior is an overreaction and tries to be less controlling, but his concern for and the palpable threats to Bella's safety limits his ability to let her go very far out of his reach. As Alice explains to Bella at the end of the novel, "Part of being a Cullen is being meticulously responsible."

Contrasted with that control is the freedom Bella feels when she is with Jacob — whether she's taking off from school on his motorcycle or hanging out by a bonfire in La Push. With that freedom comes recklessness; Jacob is impulsive, kissing her without permission or tricking her into asking him to kiss her. Ultimately with the freedom to just feel what she feels, to paraphrase Jacob, Bella makes the tricky discovery that she is in love with him.

As Bella battles to have more control over her life, her two suitors face their own battles. Jacob deals with the limitations of being part of the wolf pack, something he had "no choice" over and which he compares to being "drafted into a war you didn't know existed." Edward has had more time to develop his self-control but still battles his feelings of jealousy; he knows that hurting Jacob would upset Bella so he fights to remain in control of his less-than-gentlemanly impulses.

> *"I knew exactly what I wanted, but I was suddenly terrified of getting it."*
> Bella (Eclipse, 269)

Both Edward and Bella battle with their desire for one another. In the Twilight Saga, romantic love and sex are dangerous — Edward poses a serious physical threat to Bella every time they are together; Jacob doesn't know his own strength with Bella, kisses her against her will, and the kiss she asks for is "not far from violence"; Emily bears disfiguring scars from Sam losing control and phasing too close to her; Bella is accosted and nearly attacked by a group of men in *Twilight*; and, most viciously, Rosalie was attacked and left for dead by her fiancé and his drunken friends. Since the beginning of their romance, Edward made it clear to Bella that being physical was extremely dangerous. If he even slightly lost control, he could kill her. As the time when Bella will be turned into a vampire approaches, she realizes that she wants to lose her virginity as a human. It's the only way she can be sure she will still have the same feelings for Edward since existence as a newborn vampire is so volatile. Edward eventually

First published in 1920, American poet Robert Frost's "Fire and Ice" serves as the epigraph for *Eclipse*, and as the title of chapter 22. The poem reflects the battle between Edward's iciness and Jacob's fieriness and the conflict Bella has choosing between desire and passion or control and order – with the looming threat of her world being destroyed by Victoria's army and by Bella's own decision to become a vampire.

> "I am really surprised by the conflict between the Jacob and the Edward fans. . . . I didn't realize there was going to be such strong feelings and I'm surprised by how many people think they have to love one or the other, because it's quite easy for me to love both."
>
> – Stephenie Meyer

agrees to *try* but only after they are married; the "old-fashioned" vampire is worried that sex before marriage could endanger both of their chances of getting into heaven. Though at first she scoffs at the idea, Bella comes to believe that Edward's suggested order (marriage, sex, transforming into a vampire) is the "right" and "responsible" way for her too. Unsurprisingly, the ideas tying abstinence to virtue presented in *Eclipse*, and the rest of the Saga, align with the religious ideas that Stephenie Meyer holds dear.

Fittingly for the novel wherein Bella realizes just what it means to lose her human life and to become a vampire, *Eclipse* is the darkest and most violent of the series. With the murder spree in Seattle, the harrowing back story of Jasper's days building a newborn vampire army, the trauma that Rosalie endured as a human, and the action-packed fight scene that ends the book, Stephenie Meyer adds a level of monstrosity to *Eclipse* that was mostly left to the imagination in *Twilight* and *New Moon*. It is not only the literal monsters that raise the degree of horror; Bella comes to realize just how monstrous one person can be to another, inflicting pain and torture emotionally not physically. Bella is nothing if not empathetic, and she spends the duration of the novel feeling the pain she inflicts on Jacob by her absence and the pain she causes Edward by her love for Jacob. Both Edward and Bella blame themselves for the suffering the other endures. Bella calls herself a "hideous person" for the way she's treated Jacob, and compares herself to Medusa, the once beautiful maiden of Greek myth who, having lost her virtue and beauty, became a disgusting monster the sight of whom would turn men to stone.

Bella grows up over the course of *Eclipse* as she decides to take her head out of the proverbial sand and evaluate her choices, her feelings, and the effect her actions will have on the people (and monsters) she loves. At the outset of the novel, Charlie suggests that she find balance in her life. Though he meant she should spend more time apart from Edward, Bella does follow his advice in the end; she discovers a better way to be with Edward, negotiating compromises they both can live with, and she becomes more honest with herself and consequently more at peace with the path she chooses, knowing that she has considered her choice thoroughly. Edward says to her in the meadow, "You can have happiness your way," and by the end of *Eclipse*, Bella has figured out for herself how best to achieve that.

WUTHERING HEIGHTS

In her introduction to the Penguin Classics edition of *Wuthering Heights*, Pauline Nestor describes the novel as having a "sense of a self-enclosed, almost hermetically sealed world," a "passionate engagement with the dark and fiery world of the imagination," and "intensity and escapism [in] the novel's romance" — words that could just as suitably be used to identify what makes *Eclipse* such a captivating read for its millions of fans. Published in 1847, Emily Brontë's *Wuthering Heights* is a haunting story about the torturous romance between Heathcliff and Catherine and her other suitor, Edgar. Like *Romeo and Juliet* in *New Moon*, *Wuthering Heights* plays a key part in the narrative of *Eclipse* as Edward and Bella discuss the merits of the book and identify with, and are repulsed by, its characters.

Though HarperTeen released the classic with a Twilight-inspired cover and the tag line "Bella & Edward's favorite novel," it isn't actually Edward's favorite — far from it. He describes it as a "hate story" in which the "characters are ghastly people who ruin each other's lives." In *Wuthering Heights*, the young Heathcliff leaves the titular estate after a misunderstanding. He hears Catherine say that to marry him would be degrading; he does not hear her pledge her love for him. She falls ill

> *". . . he's more myself than I am.*
> *Whatever our souls are made of,*
> *his and mine are the same."*
>
> (Catherine, Wuthering Heights)

in his absence, like Bella in *New Moon*, and her extreme melancholic sickness changes who she is fundamentally. During his absence, Heathcliff too undergoes a transformation, returning to Wuthering Heights a man more suitable for marrying. He and Edgar, suitor to Catherine, have an innate dislike of one another, comparable to the animosity between vampire Edward and werewolf Jacob. With "eyes full of black fire," there is ferocity and cruelty in Heathcliff that borders on the monstrous. It is only his love for Catherine that stops him from murdering Edgar, whom she marries. In chapter 11 of *Eclipse*, Edward tells Bella that he can identify with some of Heathcliff's feelings and she finds the book open to the passage where Heathcliff explains to Nelly that if he had been husband to Catherine, he wouldn't have banished Edgar from his wife's company, because it would have hurt her to do so: "Had he been in my place, and I in his, though I hated him with a hatred that turned my life to gall, I never

The torn red ribbon on the cover of *Eclipse* represents the choice Bella is making to tear herself from her human life; the threads that remain attached symbolize the difficulty of making that break and leaving family, friends, and Jacob in the mortal realm.

> *"If all else perished, and he remained,*
> *I should still continue to be;*
> *and if all else remained, and he were*
> *annihilated, the universe would*
> *turn to a mighty stranger."*
>
> (Catherine, *Wuthering Heights*)

would have raised a hand against him." Edward may also have connected to the passage shortly thereafter where Heathcliff describes what his life would be without Catherine: "Two words would comprehend my future — *death* and *hell* — existence, after losing her, would be hell."

Bella compulsively re-reads the novel because she connects to its "inevitability": "How nothing can keep them apart — not her selfishness, or his evil, or even death, in the end. . . ." She points to the love between Catherine and Heathcliff as "their only redeeming quality." In one way, her commentary could be interpreted as Stephenie Meyer's own defense of her single-minded lovers; Bella and Edward are not nearly as destructive as Catherine and Heathcliff but their love brings a great deal of pain to those around them and to each other. The unprecedented intensity of their love is the single most exemplary thing about them, either as individuals or as a unit, just as Catherine and Heathcliff's love is what makes them special. After Catherine's death, Heathcliff wails that he cannot live "without his life," meaning Catherine, in the passage Edward knows by heart and recites to Bella in chapter 27, "Needs."

In the climax of *Eclipse*, Bella realizes how much pain she's inflicted on Edward and Jacob and compares herself to Catherine for being "selfish," "hurtful," for "torturing the ones" she loved. Catherine feels anguish when Heathcliff leaves her, as Bella does with Edward, and also feels confident that Edgar's love for her is unwavering, just like Jacob's feelings for Bella. Bella distinguishes between "her Jacob" and "other Jacob" (one Dr. Jekyll, one Mr. Hyde); similarly Catherine separates Heathcliff into two personas, one "hers," one not. But neither Jacob nor Heathcliff makes that distinction himself, causing misunderstandings to lead to moments of unbridled passion and near violence.

Emily Brontë's novel is set in an isolated locale where the natural world, with its brewing storms and harsh conditions, mirror the characters' emotional turmoil. Notions of sin and temptation, feverish dreams that shake one to the core, and Shakespearean allusions all color the world of *Wuthering Heights*. At the center is Heathcliff, a take-off on the Byronic hero. All of these qualities — from the unseasonal weather plaguing the Olympic Peninsula in June to the tortured Romantic hero in Edward Cullen — also shape Stephenie Meyer's *Eclipse* and help to create a novel which (to borrow Pauline Nestor's description of *Wuthering Heights*) celebrates a "transcendent love which surpasses the bounds of authority, mundanity, even death."

In the Darkness of Eclipse

For the screenplay of *Eclipse*, Stephenie Meyer became an evener greater resource for Melissa Rosenberg than she'd been on *New Moon*. Said Rosenberg, "For the third one, I gave her the outline, which I would never normally do but I know her to be such a collaborative person and she was really helpful on that. I wanted to keep her involved every step of the way. . . . It's been a really great collaboration." With the third film, the accomplished screenwriter felt she could use all the help she could get. "It was a very big challenge to write," she admits. "It was probably the greatest challenge. You wouldn't think so because there's action in the book, there's all this action, but then you realize, 'Oh, wait a minute, the action is all in the back half. What's happening in the front?' . . . I did get to use [Stephenie's] mythology even more, so there's going to be some great what we would call Easter eggs, if you were doing a DVD, of some of her mythology that gets to be on the screen that wasn't able to be in the book."

As with *Twilight* and *New Moon*, there were certain things that the author was adamant be retained in the film version, and everyone was happy to oblige — since they agreed completely. "What we're going to see in *Eclipse*," explained Rosenberg, "is this triangle between Bella, Edward, and Jacob, and I think we're going to see a lot of heat between these characters. Jacob has been so well established now in *New Moon*; he's a real rival for Edward, and so I think he's going to throw that relationship into a bit of upheaval. We had to have the tent scene. This is one of Stephenie's favorite chapters in all the books she's written. . . . With Jacob keeping Bella

159

warm, it's just this incredibly tense scene but finally these two guys are talking to each other and it's a really interesting conversation."

At the director's helm for *Eclipse* was David Slade, a British filmmaker whose career began directing music videos, including three for Meyer's favorite band, Muse. In 2006, he made his feature film debut with *Hard Candy*, a thriller about a teenage girl (played by Ellen Page) and an older man, which was well reviewed. The next year he was back working with dark material directing the gruesome

horror film *30 Days of Night*, an adaptation from a graphic novel series of the same name about an isolated Alaskan town besieged by vicious vampires. Fittingly David Slade is directing the darkest of the Twilight Saga series. Said Summit Entertainment's Erik Feig, "Stephenie Meyer's *Eclipse* is a muscular, rich, vivid book and we at Summit looked long and hard for a director who could do it justice. We believe we have found that talent in David Slade, a director who has been able to create complex, visually arresting worlds. We cannot

wait to see the *Eclipse* he brings to life and brings to the fans eagerly awaiting its arrival in summer of 2010."

Slade's actors were as enthusiastic as the studio executives. While promoting *The Runaways* at Sundance in January 2010, Kristen Stewart said, "He's a very technical director. Very. Very. He's very thoughtful. I think it's going to be cool for *Twilight*, like, shotwise. He's very conceptual. He really, really takes a lot of time to . . . you're not going to see, like, a bunch of Steadicam. It's very deliberate,

"[*Eclipse* is] a massively different movie to *New Moon*. There's so many more main parts, and having these huge battle sequences – I've never done anything like it in any of the other movies."

– Robert Pattinson

A huge set-up to film a scene where newborn vampires emerge from the water.

162

The *Eclipse* crew takes over a Vancouver street to set up a crane shot.

which is very cool. It gives you more time to think about what you're doing." Newcomer to the Saga, Xavier Samuel (who plays Victoria's henchman Riley), commented, "It seems like David has approached it very differently to the previous directors — I think he's really embracing the darker side of it, which is really cool. He's über intelligent, [a] very technically astute director." Charlie "Demetri" Bewley agreed with his fellow vampire: "David is a master of mood. *Eclipse* has this different mood about it; it's dark and vicious. You get to see the brutal nature of vampires and what they are really capable of, which is something we haven't really seen in the first two movies." Going on to compare him to Chris Weitz, Bewley noted, "They are very different directors. David understands what each scene needs — absolute fine tuning. He might stop the scene halfway

> "I think what I really love about *Eclipse*, what was interesting for me to explore, was different levels of love and acknowledging that the ideals that you maybe had a little while ago aren't true. Bella is innately honest. That's something that I feel she is. In *Eclipse* she lies to herself and she lies to everyone around her about the fact that she's in love with Jacob, just not as much. It's not that extra thing that you can't really even describe."
>
> – Kristen Stewart

through and just tweak something before saying, 'Go back, say that word again and I want you to put the emphasis on *that*.' *Eclipse* is going to be more real."

Part of making it more "real" for the Cullens was a great deal of physical preparation for the big final battle. Ashley Greene told *Entertainment Tonight* that to prepare for *Eclipse*, she had a month of fight and stunt training, as well as intensive two-a-day workouts. "Learning to run and jump off walls and land on people's shoulders, flips, and just throwing your body in ways that under no circumstance you would normally do," detailed Ashley, who has a lot to live up to in Alice's fighting style which is described in *Eclipse* as dancing — "spiraling and twisting and curling in on herself" with "graceful patterns." Up for the challenge, Ashley was bruised but having fun: "It will look really, really good by the time we get to the fight sequence [with the newborn vampire army]. . . . They're trying to make us look like we know what we're doing."

For Taylor Lautner, moving from *New Moon* to *Eclipse* was a much easier transition than from *Twilight* to *New Moon*. He was eager to get on to filming *Eclipse*, which is his favorite in the Twilight Saga because "you have Edward and Jacob teaming up to protect Bella. And then there's the love triangle among all three of them. I think that's the ultimate high point of the series." Just like series' creator Stephenie Meyer, Taylor's "favorite scene is the tent scene where the three of us are together. And it's going to be really funny. There's a lot of comedy in *Eclipse*."

Being Bella in *Eclipse* meant a new set of challenges for Kristen Stewart. "Bella is back to being herself," says Kristen. "She's comfortable and self-assured in a way that she wasn't in *New Moon*. But in *Eclipse*, she lies to herself and she lies to everyone around her about the fact that she's in love with Jacob." The prospect of playing that conflicted character and watching the complications unfold in the story excited the young actress. "I'm actually looking

> "... in *Eclipse*, the proposal when they're on the bed, yes — to me, that was a quintessential scene from the book. When Edward gets on his knees, with his mother's ring, and she says yes — that was one of the most romantic scenes that Stephenie wrote in all four books."
> — Melissa Rosenberg

forward to seeing the love triangle actually become a huge problem. We sort of innocently touch on it in *New Moon*, but it actually becomes something that is very, very real. . . . I've always backed [Bella] up in her, like, ultimate devotion to Edward and to see that falter will be interesting." She wasn't the only one. Asked what he was most excited about in *Eclipse*, Robert Pattinson quipped, "Bella's little bit of treachery. I think that will be a good scene." As for his approach to portraying Edward, Robert said, "I liked the still parts of *Twilight*. So I did that again [in *New Moon*]. For the third one, I've kind of, you know, tried to loosen it up a bit again."

Principal photography for *Eclipse* began on August 18, 2009, once again in Vancouver, British Columbia, where the cast was now being followed on a daily basis by paparazzi and fans. Though there was a new director on board, the *New Moon* cinematographer, Javier Aguirresarobe (or the "sartorial Spaniard" as Slade lovingly dubbed him), returned to provide continuity in the visual approach. David Slade provided fans too far away for set visits with updates through his Twitter account, posting beautiful portraits of the crew and tidbits about the progress of shooting. When it

came time to film the Forks High graduation scene, it was Kristen Stewart who was eager to share her story of the coincidental timing of her matriculation with Bella's. She was "a little late. I was 19 when I graduated high school." But while on set filming graduation, Kristen realized she could take advantage of her costume: "It was a trip. It was the week that I'd finished my last assignment and I got all my credits. I made an extra go backstage with me and take a picture of me in my cap and gown — the extra that gave me the diploma. And I shook his hand and looked at the camera — so I have my own graduation photo."

The shoot was intensive and at the end of it, David Slade posted on Twitter, "Twilight Eclipse officially wrapped shooting, at 4.30 am October 29th. Physically and emotionally exhausted." But his work was not over: after production comes the intensive process of post-production where the film is shaped from hours and hours of footage into one cohesive whole. Slade let Twilight fans in on the progress as *Eclipse* took its form in the editing process. Posted Slade, "Edward seems to be a really strong presence, the intensity of the love story & rivalry between Jacob is in the driving seat"; "Jacob & Bella are matching

> **"There's a very big battle and I'm really looking forward to seeing that as directed by David Slade who I know is going to do a great job."**
>
> – Melissa Rosenberg

with intensity, & it's all even with the action sequences. Right now we are in a great state of balance"; "Edit getting finer and finer, film now running at a great length. Lots of SFX work to do but we feel good"; "Onwards we cut, I am watching the great Art Jones tighten our edit, poor Jacob is on his broken rib bed, raining outside, lunch soon." Film editor Art Jones had also worked with Slade on his previous two features, *Hard Candy* and *30 Days of Night*. Because *New Moon* had been such a great box office success, Summit Entertainment decided that *Eclipse* would not only be widely released on June 30, but it would be in IMAX theaters as well so Twilighters could see it on the *really* big screen.

With the stunning sales and critical acclaim the first two soundtracks received, artists were keen to get on the soundtrack for *Eclipse*, which Chop Shop Records would once again be in charge of putting together. Adam Lambert, The National Rifle, Lee Safar, Candace Charee, and Tegan and Sara among others made pitches to be included. As had been the case with *Twilight* and *New Moon*, a new composer was enlisted to score the film: Howard Shore. Three-time Academy Award winner (for the Lord of the Films trilogy), four-time Grammy winner, and two-time Golden Globe winner, the Canadian composer's work has been described by *Movie Score Magazine* as "dark, brooding, and elegant."

chapter 19

The
Eclipse Army

BRYCE DALLAS HOWARD
AS VICTORIA

❀ ❀ ❀

Bryce Dallas Howard was born into a showbiz family on March 2, 1981, but her parents, writer Cheryl and esteemed actor-director Ron Howard, didn't push their children into the business. For a long time, the L.A.-native didn't even want to be an actress, and she admits, "Telling everyone I wanted to go into forensic anthropology was my form of rebellion." But her godfather, Henry Winkler (who will always be known to *Happy Days* fans as "The Fonz"), knew better, saying she "was destined to act."

Bryce developed her acting at NYU's Tisch School of the Arts, focusing on theater. She earned a starring role in the school's production of *Hamletmachine*, which attracted her an agent. Enough work followed that she didn't actually finish her degree; her big break came from a fateful performance as Rosalind in *As You Like It*. Bryce wasn't even supposed to play the role, but the original Rosalind went to L.A. to film a pilot. "It was so by chance," says Bryce. "You just never know what your life is going to look like." That night, writer-director M. Night Shyamalan saw her performance and knew he'd found his Ivy Walker for *The Village* (2004). He told his production team, "There's this girl, I don't want to audition her, I just want to offer her the part." Looking back Bryce notes, "It was so ridiculous and surreal. It was this dream of every actor, being discovered."

Though she also appeared in *Book of Love* (2004), her next major role was in Lars von Trier's *Manderlay* (2005), picking up the role of Grace Mulligan from Nicole Kidman's portrayal in 2003's *Dogville*. Interestingly, this role also came from the same run of *As You Like It*; a friend of *Manderlay*'s producer had also been enchanted by the actress.

In 2006 she worked again with Shyamalan in *Lady in the Water*, playing the titular water nymph. She also reprised her role of Rosalind for a filmed version of *As You Like It* by renowned Shakespearian actor-director Kenneth Branagh, which earned her a Golden Globe nomination.

The following year Bryce appeared in *The Loss of a Teardrop Diamond*, based on a forgotten screenplay by famed playwright Tennessee Williams. The formally trained actress also proved herself adept at more commercial fare, joining the Spider-Man franchise for its third installment to play Gwen Stacy, and in *Terminator Salvation* as Kate Connor (a role formerly played by Claire Danes).

But it was her third round of picking up a character from another actress that proved the most difficult, when she accepted the role of Victoria in *Eclipse*, filling the place of Rachelle Lefevre after her hotly contested dismissal. Fans protested the switch out of loyalty to Rachelle and a desire to preserve continuity across the three films. But Summit held firm and exec Erik Feig announced, "We are incredibly happy that Bryce has agreed to come into the franchise. Rachelle brought Victoria to great screen life and Bryce will bring a new dimension to the character. The franchise is lucky to have such a talented actress as Bryce coming in to fill the role."

In a tight place, Bryce expressed her sympathy. "Rachelle really created an incredible character and is exquisite. I feel like the uproar that occurred was really appropriate," she said. "You've seen the actors grow with the franchise." The actress was also quick to reaffirm her dedication to the project: "I've read the books and loved the books from the very beginning and these characters are extraordinary. It's such an absorbing story that I just felt very lucky, given the unfortunate circumstances surrounding it, that I was just invited in." Her fellow cast members were sorry to see Rachelle go, but welcomed Bryce with open arms. Of the fan fallout says Nikki Reed, "Bryce is handling it like a champion. She's beautiful, talented, and a wonderful addition." Playing the vengeful vamp will be an abrupt shift for an actress who admits, "I've been told over and over again that I have a kind of innocence, and I have no control over it." Yet the actress's stellar track record and the faith of her co-stars make a convincing argument for her ability to play Victoria.

Five years earlier when she was picking up the role from Nicole Kidman, Bryce demonstrated a perspective well beyond her years and one that still holds true: "It's a tremendous opportunity, and I'm eternally grateful, but it's just a certain part of my life. It's my career. Wherever that leads, in the end you're left with yourself."

KIRSTEN PROUT
AS LUCY

❀ ❀ ❀

Born September 28, 1990, and raised in Vancouver, British Columbia, Kirsten Prout fell in love with Disney films as a child, and decided she wanted to be a princess. She explains, "It was just that desire to be a character, to be someone else." She begged her parents to let her get into acting, and like many others, started with commercial work, which she did until

when she was cast as Abigail "Abby" Miller, sidekick to superhero Elektra in the 2005 action film starring Jennifer Garner. Kirsten already had the tae kwon do skills she needed, having earned her red belt. Television success followed when Kirsten landed a starring role on ABC Family's *Kyle XY* as girl-next-door Amanda Bloom. Since it was filmed in her hometown, Kirsten attended regular school for the show's three seasons. Kirsten was cast in *Eclipse* as Lucy, a bad vamp who helped Maria create a newborn army. The role suited her: "I feel a magnetic attraction to darker roles. I really like the challenge." A year of studying at McGill University in Montreal was an experience she's described as "humbling . . . I grew up on sets where I was treated like I was 25, allowed to make decisions for myself. It makes you think you know what you're doing. In university you're in classes with incredibly intelligent people — you realize you're not an expert on everything." But with so much acting work coming her way, she's putting school on hold to head back to set.

JODELLE FERLAND
AS BREE

❋ ❋ ❋

Born October 9, 1994, in Nanaimo, British Columbia, Jodelle Micah Ferland was acting before most kids even knew what acting was. She started at age two, and by four she gave a performance in the TV movie *Mermaids* that made her the youngest person ever to earn a Daytime Emmy nomination. She's been in over 40 productions in a decade — like *Cold Squad*, *Supernatural*, *Stargate SG-1*, *Smallville*, and

age 10. After gaining more varied experience with *The Dead Zone*, *Stargate SG-1*, TV movie *Once Upon a Christmas* and its sequel, the young actress (pictured above) got her big break the Stephen King miniseries *Kingdom Hospital* — but she's best known for her starring role as Sharon/Alessa in 2006 horror film *Silent Hill*. She was also in 2007's *The Messengers* with Kristen Stewart. Jodelle admits that she was a latecomer to the Twilight phenomenon, and blames it on being homeschooled. But once she was introduced to *Twilight* and the part of newborn vampire Bree came her way, she didn't hesitate for a second. "Usually I read the script before I take a role, but I haven't read this one," she said. "It's *Twilight*, of course I'm going to take it."

CATALINA SANDINO MORENO
AS MARIA

✲ ✲ ✲

Though her acting career is only a few years old, Catalina Sandino Moreno is one of three actors in the Twilight Saga to have received nods from the Academy; in fact, she earned a nomination in 2004 for her very first role. Catalina played a young, pregnant Columbian drug mule in Joshua Marston's *Maria Full of Grace*. The actress, born April 19, 1981, in Bogotá, Colombia, to a middle-class family, was studying advertising and taking a few drama classes to help combat her shyness when someone told her about the audition. She beat out over 900 hopefuls for the starring role, and the director remembers, "She was very creative — it didn't feel like someone who was trying to act. I felt like I was watching the real person." Catalina moved to New York, where she waited three years for the next promising role: "Anyone can be a beautiful girl. Any girl can do that. It does not interest me." She found worthwhile parts in *Fast Food Nation* (2006),

Paris, je t'aime (2007), Ethan Hawke's *The Hottest State, Love in the Time of Cholera* (2007), and in the two-part biopic *Che*. She joins the Twilight Saga as Maria, the vampire who turned Jasper. From being the first Colombian to receive an

Oscar nomination to being part of a massively successful franchise, the entire acting experience has been surreal for the actress: "Everything that has happened to me is so crazy. It's like a fairytale, you know?"

JULIA JONES
AS LEAH CLEARWATER

❊ ❊ ❊

Playing Leah, the broken-hearted lone female werewolf is Boston-native Julia Jones, born January 23, 1981. Julia debuted in the 2003 modeling flick *The Look*, and went on to appear in several films, before landing a recurring role on *ER* as Dr. Kaya Montoya. Julia heard about the part of Leah because of a longstanding relationship with *Eclipse*'s casting director, and nabbed an audition with David Slade. She describes bitter pack member Leah as "really alone and out there and heartbroken at the same time. And it makes her very angry and mean, and really she's just in a lot of pain and she doesn't know how to ask for help so she lashes out." Looking back on when she was cast, Julia recognized at that moment her career was phasing dramatically. "My heart started beating fast, it's a very unusual thing," says the actress, "but I think on some level I think I sort of felt like I knew that this was going to be something important and probably life-changing."

Julia's other blockbuster film was due out only 12 days before *Eclipse*. Julia was once again in the realm of the supernatural playing Cassie in comic book–adaptation *Jonah Hex*, which stars Megan Fox and Josh Brolin.

BOO BOO STEWART
AS SETH CLEARWATER

❊ ❊ ❊

For many members of the Twilight Saga cast, stunts are the most challenging part of filming, but for Boo Boo Stewart it's a piece of cake; he's been practicing martial arts since age three, and has already done credited stunts in several films, including the big budget epic *Beowulf*. Born on January 21, 1994, in Beverly Hills, California, Boo Boo's real name is Nils Allen Stewart Jr., but Boo Boo was a nickname that stuck from childhood. The actor made his big screen debut in the 2004 comedy *Yard Sale*. He beefed up his résumé with roles in *American Cowslip*, *ER*, *Everybody Hates Chris*, and *Blue Dolphin Kids* (as a host). Not just an actor and stunt double, Boo Boo proved that he could sing and dance too, as a member of the Walt Disney Records group T-Squad, which toured with Miley Cyrus and the Jonas Brothers — a good preparation for the fan-demonium that would ensue when he signed on to *Eclipse*. Boo Boo describes his character, Seth Clearwater, as "the type of guy who walks into the room and will just make you happy." In 2010, Boo Boo took on yet another job on a film set, producing as well as acting in *Logan*, and appears opposite Mira Sorvino in the family drama *Smitty*.

XAVIER SAMUEL
AS RILEY

❊ ❊ ❊

Joining the Twilight cast for *Eclipse* as Riley, the ruthless leader of Victoria's army, is the

baby-faced Xavier Samuel, born December 10, 1983, in Adelaide, Australia. The actor got his start on Aussie TV drama *McLeod's Daughters*,

and went on to make his silver screen debut in the indie drama *2:37*. Xavier showcased his talent on the stage while he continued to land sporadic film and TV work in the Land Down Under, though it was the part of Riley that would bring Xavier big recognition on the international scene. Xavier called filming the David Slade sequel "pretty intensive" and got into the physicality of the immortals, telling *9 News*, "It's a really action-packed film and I had a really great time running around on wires and learning how to fight like a vampire — however that is." Before the movie was even released, the newly in-demand actor was seeing more scripts come his way; *Twilight*'s bite has given him an unmistakable sparkle.

chapter 20

Happily Ever Afterlife

Before its release, the anticipation for *Breaking Dawn*, the last book in the Twilight Saga, was at a fever pitch, and only the range of reactions fans and critics had after reading it could match that level of intensity. *Entertainment Weekly* opined, "Meyer takes her supernatural love story several bizarre steps too far. . . . [Bella] is not only hard to identify with but positively horrifying"; the online post of that review generated over 1,500 comments arguing both sides of the debate. The *Washington Post* said, "Meyer has put a stake through the heart of her own beloved creation," and *Publishers Weekly* outlined its problem with the book: "Essentially, everyone gets everything they want, even if their desires necessitate an about-face in characterization or the messy introduction of some back story. Nobody has to renounce anything or suffer more than temporarily." On the pro–*Breaking Dawn* side, it was argued that there was nothing wrong with a happily-ever-after ending, especially when it had been hinted at and built toward since *Twilight*. After all, Bella had already survived James, Laurent, and Victoria; a vampire boyfriend and a shapeshifting best friend; two brushes with the Volturi; and found true and requited love in the process. It wasn't too risky of a bet to wager that all the loose threads of *Eclipse* would be tied up neatly by the end of *Breaking Dawn*.

The most difficult transition, for both Bella and the reader, was that from human to vampire. In the first three books, Bella was loveably human, and consequently easy to identify with. Securing the devotion of Edward, an angel on earth who sees her like she "was the prize rather than the lucky winner," removed Bella from her "every-girl" persona. The events of *Breaking Dawn* pushed her further away from common experience. Bella has a perfect wedding; a mind-blowing, if physically dangerous, first time with Edward; and a rapidly progressing vampire pregnancy — and that's all *before* she becomes a vampire possessing speed, agility, heightened senses, and her very own special power. Switching to a narrator other than Bella in Book 2, Stephenie Meyer is able to voice some of the disbelief a reader might feel by using Jacob's sarcastic perspective. As he describes at the opening of chapter 10, "I felt like — like I don't know what. Like this wasn't real. Like I was in some Goth version of a bad sitcom." Meyer returns to Bella's perspective just as Jacob's might become uncomfortable for

Stephenie Meyer explained the symbolism of the final Twilight Saga cover on her website: "*Breaking Dawn*'s cover is a metaphor for Bella's progression throughout the entire saga. She began as the weakest (at least physically, when compared to vampires and werewolves) player on the board: the pawn. She ended as the strongest: the queen. In the end, it's Bella that brings about the win for the Cullens."

readers; he imprints on Renesmee as Bella begins her transformation into a vampire, and the reader gets to see those first moments, as well as the rest of the action, through Bella's new extra-perceptive vampire eyes.

A central theme in *Breaking Dawn*, and the series as a whole, is the power of love. In *Eclipse*, Bella discovered that she could love both Jacob and Edward, but in vastly different ways, and in *Breaking Dawn*, Bella learns a whole new kind — maternal love for Renesmee. She refuses to have an abortion despite the fatal risk the pregnancy poses, because Bella already has a strong maternal bond with her fetus — perhaps because of its rapid development and Renesmee's special way of communicating. The disconnect between the logical course of action, which Edward and Carlisle campaign for, and the one Bella takes, since she is guided by her emotions, has been part of the Saga since *Twilight*. Making a similar choice just a year and a half earlier, Bella decided to be with Edward despite the threat he posed to her. In chapter 7 of *Breaking Dawn*, Bella describes her new wealth of feeling: "There was no division — my love was not split between [Edward and Renesmee] now; it wasn't like that. It was more like my heart had grown, swollen up to twice its size."

First by "protecting" Renesmee in her womb and then by protecting the Renesmee-supporting witnesses with her shield, Bella embodies the role of guardian in *Breaking Dawn*. In the Twiverse, humans who become vampires have their personality traits heightened in their new state — Jasper's charisma turned into the ability to alter moods, Edward's empathy became an ability to read minds, and Bella's self-control and need for privacy turns into the ability to cast a protective shield over herself and others. Her unprecedented control as a newborn vampire allows her to triumph as the "superhero of the day," as Alice puts it, in the showdown with the Volturi at the end of *Breaking Dawn*.

As a vampire, Bella not only gains the physical capability to stand ready to fight against those who threaten her family, but is finally on equal footing with Edward. In *Eclipse*, the two learned to compromise, but it takes more than their marriage vows to make them equals in their partnership. Once Bella is out of physical danger and Edward no longer needs to protect her, the balance that was lacking in their relationship is finally achieved. In their marriage, they are sealed to one another and to their family for eternity, a concept Stephenie Meyer drew from Mormonism. Says Garrett of the Cullens, "I have witnessed the bonds within this family — I say *family* and not *coven*. These strange golden-eyed ones deny their very natures. But in return have they found something worth even more, perhaps, than mere gratification of desire?"

Though the Volturi may return someday, *Breaking Dawn* has a decidedly happy ending: Bella escaped the usual wildness of being a newborn vampire, Renesmee is safe and will live forever with Jacob at her side, Alice and Jasper never abandoned their family, Charlie has found love with Sue Clearwater and is able to be both father to Bella and grandfather to Renesmee, Edward and Jacob are at peace and have a familial bond, and after so much struggle and restraint Edward and Bella are now free to be at each other's side "forever and forever and forever."

A MIDSUMMER NIGHT'S DREAM

For a book of *Breaking Dawn*'s length, it's fitting that Stephenie Meyer drew inspiration from not one but two Shakespearian works: *The Merchant of Venice* and *A Midsummer Night's Dream* (published in 1600). Like *Breaking Dawn*, *A Midsummer Night's Dream* opens with a wedding approaching: both Edward and Bella's and Theseus and Hippolyta's "nuptial hour / Draws on apace." Theseus, the Duke of Athens, is interested in celebrating appropriately; Alice's wedding planning echoes his desire to have all the "pomp" befitting the occasion. The Duke is called upon to hear out

Egeus whose daughter, Hermia, refuses to marry the man he has chosen for her, Demetrius, because she is in love with Lysander. Like Bella, Hermia has "Turn'd her obedience" from her father to marry her suitor. The triangle of Lysander, Hermia, and Demetrius — one man favored, the other persistent — is echoed in the Edward, Bella, and Jacob relationship as well as in the strained dynamic between Emily, Sam, and Leah. In the famous line, Lysander urges Hermia to bear this trial with patience for "the course of true love never did run smooth." The lovers decide to elope. Hermia is willing to give up her home, father, and friends to live with Lysander outside of Athens. Though Bella agrees to a traditional wedding, she is also making the same sacrifices for her life with Edward.

Unbeknownst to the mortals in *A Midsummer Night's Dream* a parallel and magical world inhabited by fairies is right under their noses. The closely guarded secrecy of the vampire and shapeshifter world in the Twilight Saga parallels the supernatural one in Shakespeare's play; the fairies are free to toy with the humans, but the humans remain unaware of the forces that work upon them. There is discord between Oberon, the king of the fairies, and Titania, the queen, over a "loved boy" — a human child who has been brought into the mystical realm. Like Renesmee — a creature with partly human origins but supernatural qualities who is the focus of the Volturi's attention — the boy is "so sweet a changeling" that Titania "makes him all her joy" and she refuses to give him over to Oberon.

Further complicating the lovers' story is

"Now do I wish it, love it, long for it, And will for evermore be true to it."
(Demetrius, A Midsummer Night's Dream)

Helena, best friend to Hermia and once the beloved of Demetrius. Just as Sam ditched Leah for Emily, Helena has been cast aside by Demetrius as he pursues Hermia. Like Jacob's and Leah's ongoing bitterness at being rejected, Helena is envious of Hermia's charms and wishes there could be equality in her and Demetrius's affections but instead must "love unlov'd." Oberon sees the conflict between the four mortal lovers and asks Puck, his mischief-making fairy, to use the "love-in-idleness" flower to change Demetrius's affections from Hermia to Helena. As with imprinting, there is no choice in the object of one's love once this juice has been administered. In a mistake for comedic effect, both Lysander and Demetrius have their affection turned to Helena. Though both men love her because of the flower, Oberon makes a distinction — "Some true love turn'd, and not a false turn'd true" — between the false love Lysander feels for Helena and the restored true love Demetrius feels for her. In *A Midsummer Night's Dream* as in *Breaking Dawn*, there are certain pairings that are presented as "right" and "true" (Edward and Bella, Jacob and Renesmee) and others that were not meant to be (Bella and Jacob). As dawn breaks in *A Midsummer Night's Dream*, the four lovers awake, having found requited love, and they will "eternally be knit" in marriage.

Book 3's epigraph was written by Orson Scott Card, one of Stephenie Meyer's favorite writers. The passage, taken from the 2006 novel *Empire*, encapsulates the torment Bella and the Cullens undergo as they are held hostage waiting for their trial with the Volturi.

For Book 2's epigraph, Stephenie Meyer selected a quotation from the clownish artisan Bottom: "And yet, to say the truth, reason and love keep little company together nowadays." The irrationality of love and the wild behavior it incites feature prominently in both Shakespeare's and Meyer's tales. The switching affections nearly lead the *Midsummer* lovers to physical altercation while Jacob finds the focus of his affection shifting dramatically from Bella to her daughter with one glance at the newborn. Almost as unlikely as the regal Titania falling for the donkey-headed Bottom, Jacob experiences firsthand the distance between love and reason when he imprints on Renesmee and his fierce devotion to the child erases his romantic interest in Bella. The theme of allegiance and the sometimes-conflicting claims of romantic love, family, and friendship, are explored in both the play and *Breaking Dawn*.

Bottom says to his fellow actors as they rehearse their play for the Duke's wedding, "we must leave the killing out," and Stephenie Meyer followed that tradition in crafting the ending for the Twilight Saga (with the exception of Irina's death) — requited love between the young couples, mature love for Charlie and Sue Clearwater (a parallel to Theseus and Hippolyta), and order restored in the mystical world. Meyer models her harmonious ending on the "gentle concord" found in the final scenes of *A Midsummer Night's Dream*.

THE MERCHANT OF VENICE

William Shakespeare's comedy *The Merchant of Venice* (also published in 1600) is the subject of much debate and controversy, mostly surrounding its anti-Semitic characterization of Shylock, the money-lender and villain in the play's action. In *Breaking Dawn*, the book in the Twilight Saga that divided the fandom, Stephenie Meyer has Alice select Bella's copy of this play in which to write her farewell — a tip-off to readers that *The Merchant of Venice* influenced the final book in the series.

At the outset of the play, Portia finds herself still under the control of her father who in his will decreed the manner in which she could marry. Suitors must choose from one of three caskets (gold, silver, or lead) each bearing a riddle; the right one contains her picture and grants the chooser Portia's hand. Just as an imprinted Quileute is without the will to deny the ties binding him to his beloved, Portia has no choice over who her husband will be. The right suitor will prove his worthiness by his ability to solve the riddle. Says

MY SPARKLING VAMPIRE

The basics are the same – an immortal blood-drinking creature who used to be human – but the vampires in Stephenie Meyer's Twilight Saga are a whole new breed from those which preceded them in myth, literature, and popular culture.

- Undoubtedly the characteristic that's received the most attention: in sunshine, Twilight vampires don't burn; they sparkle.
- No retractable fangs for Edward, but his kind still have razor-sharp teeth.
- Garlic, holy water, and crosses cannot be used to keep a vampire at bay in the Twiverse.
- Most vampires need an invite before they can step foot into a human's dwelling, but Edward proves that rule doesn't hold. He could pop in uninvited to watch Bella sleep whenever he wanted.
- A vampire's eyes change color according to what they've been feeding on and how recently: red for a human-blood drinker (or a newborn), black for a hungry vegetarian vamp, and amber for a well-fed Cullen.
- Though they have super speed and strength as well as enhanced senses and reflexes, Meyer's vampires aren't magic. They can't transform into bats, other creatures, or spooky fog.
- The Cullens don't sleep in coffins. They don't sleep at all!
- Stephenie's vampires may not be the first to be cold to the touch, but having literally rock-hard bodies was a new concept for the genre.
- There is only one rule among vampires: to keep their existence a secret.
- Throw away your stakes, slayers. These vampires can't be killed by a wooden stake through the heart, or by exposure to daylight. Instead they have to be beheaded, dismembered, and burned.
- The idea of a "good vampire" didn't originate with Dr. Carlisle Cullen. Recent pop culture bloodsuckers who also live the vegetarian lifestyle include *Buffy*'s "vampire with a soul" Angel, *True Blood*'s Bill Compton, and *The Vampire Diaries'* Stefan Salvatore.
- And finally, perhaps most shockingly of all, they play baseball!

Portia, the "lott'ry of my destiny / Bars me the right of voluntary choosing." Portia is bound in her duty to her father, and though she dislikes the arrangement, she nevertheless follows his wishes. Bella, on the other hand, is bound in other ways — as a human, she is weaker than Edward and his family, and to become a vampire, she must first marry Edward. She decides to break the familial bond she has to Charlie (as well as to Renee, Jacob, and her human friends). In that way she mimics the choice that Jessica, daughter of Shylock, makes in eloping with her true love, Lorenzo. Jessica is eager to no longer be of her father's "blood," but to be of her would-be husband's, a Christian. Analogously, Bella is willing to lose the blood-ties she has to Charlie and instead have Edward's vampire venom course through her veins.

Jacob's temperament in the pre-Renesmee portion of *Breaking Dawn* is like that of Antonio, dear and loyal friend to Bassanio, who enters into the famous pound-of-flesh bond with Shylock in order that Bassanio may travel to Belmont and woo Portia. Despite the risk to himself, Antonio is unwaveringly supportive of his friend but has a melancholic temperament, describing the world as a "stage where every man must play a part, / And mine a sad one." Unlike Antonio who doesn't know why he's depressed, Jacob is well aware of the cause of his distress — the woman he loves is marrying a vampire and then becoming one herself. Antonio's actions are noble; he is willing to endanger himself for a loved one. Jacob also demonstrates that capacity, by leaving the wolf pack behind in order to protect Bella and her family.

The climax of the conflict in *Breaking Dawn* is closely modeled on *The Merchant of Venice*'s trial with Shylock. At the crux of the problem is an antagonist who hides his true motivation — personal gain and revenge — behind a mask, who spouts undeniable truths about the

Surprising Bella in chapter 27, Renesmee reads the mariners' song from Alfred Tennyson's "The Lotos-Eaters" (1832), a poem based on an episode in Homer's *Odyssey* in which the wearied Trojan warriors desire to rest.

importance of abiding by rules in a society. Shylock is interested in weeding out Antonio from Venetian business and has "an ancient grudge" against him; Aro wants to weaken the astonishing strength of the Cullens and take the gifted vampires into his clan to bolster the Volturi's might. Like Bella's wariness as Aro shifts his attention from the "immortal child" issue to the unknowable danger Renesmee *could* pose to the vampire world, Bassanio expresses his reluctance that Antonio enter into the bond with Shylock: "I like not fair terms and a villain's mind." Antonio and his friends hold the moral ground against Shylock, as the Cullens and their supporters do against the Volturi. Both trials — Antonio's in act four and the meeting in the clearing in *Breaking Dawn* — turn on the question of being merciful. Eager to profit from the perceived misstep the Cullens have made with their "immortal child," Aro takes the same stance as Shylock: "Tell me not of mercy." It is only when the Volturi find themselves outmaneuvered, primarily by Bella, that they, like Shylock, scurry away defeated.

Bella's journey in *Breaking Dawn* mirrors Portia's in *The Merchant of Venice*: both are bound to certain roles but are able, through marriage, to prove their smarts and capabilities by resolving the central conflict peacefully. When Bassanio chooses the right casket and proves his love for her, Portia (who luckily loves him back) is freed from her father's bond and becomes the true mistress of her estate, marrying Bassanio immediately. Hearing of Antonio's impending trial with Shylock, she sends Bassanio to his side and quickly hatches her own ingenious plot to resolve the case in

"For, having such a blessing in his lady He finds the joys of heaven here on earth."
(Jessica, The Merchant of Venice)

Antonio's favor. Portia must first shed her identity as a woman, putting on the costume of a doctor of laws and temporarily becoming a man, so that her wisdom will be given fair hearing in court. Bella must also shed her identity — that of a human in a permanent transformation to a vampire — in order to fully realize her potential. Both women wisely and actively intervene in the action to resolve the conflict; Portia outwits Shylock and Bella outplays the Volturi. Says the Duke of Venice to the disguised Portia, after her triumph over Shylock, "I never knew so young a body with so old a head," a description that brings to mind Renee's characterization of Bella as her "middle-aged child."

The Merchant of Venice ends with three happily married couples — Jessica and Lorenzo, Nerissa and Graziano, and Portia and Bassanio — just as *Breaking Dawn* has its own happily ever after for the Cullen clan, which now includes Bella, Renesmee, and Jacob. Lorenzo's words in the final act of the play fittingly describe the loving bonds that tie each couple and the family together: "Such harmony is in immortal souls."

FILMING THE IMPOSSIBLE

As soon as *Breaking Dawn* was published in August 2008, both its author and its readers wondered how on earth a filmmaker would be

able to adapt the 756-page novel that featured a racy, furniture-and-pillow-destroying honeymoon; a graphic vampire cesarean section; a half-human, half-vampire developmentally accelerated infant; and a wolf pack who communicates telepathically . . . among other complex situations. Wrote Stephenie Meyer on her website, "When I said that *Breaking Dawn* might be impossible to film, it's because of Renesmee. . . . I've never seen a CGI human being who truly looks real. An actress can't play Renesmee, at least not when she's a few days old; she's the size of a baby, but her expressions are totally controlled and aware. She would have to be a construct, and CGI isn't quite there yet. Of course, they develop amazing new technologies everyday, and we've got a little time left."

For Melissa Rosenberg, the screenwriter who had successfully translated the first three books into screenplays, reading *Breaking Dawn* for the first time was just as shocking an experience as it was for fans of the series: "Every time I turn the page I'm like, 'Wow, she is really going there?!' She just took the reins off. It's like the first three books were restraint, restraint, restraint and suddenly

she's going hog wild. It's such a bold thing to do, for a writer of a beloved series to go, 'This is my world and I'm taking it here. I'm pulling the doors back and letting everyone look in.' It's incredibly satisfying after these books full of mystery." As early as April 2009, Rosenberg was asked by Summit Entertainment, who had the foresight to license all four books when they picked up *Twilight*, to "re-read it and start thinking about it," despite the fact that the official announcement that *Breaking Dawn* was greenlit had not yet been made nearly a year later.

One point of discussion Melissa Rosenberg did not anticipate being a problem was the mature content of the book. Explained the writer, "You have to know your audience. And . . . there's no reason for it not to be . . . PG-13." Reflecting back on the contents of the novel, she continued, "If I were to be writing [the *Breaking Dawn* script], I think there are many things that probably are inappropriate, and there are probably other things that can be implied. I don't think that it will be a problem."

A big debate in the fandom, and at Summit Entertainment, was whether *Breaking Dawn* should be split into two films, as *Harry Potter*

"I don't know, I think that would be crazy. . . .
Uh, selectively maybe. Maybe certain scenes. . . . You don't want
Renesmee to be scary, you don't want her to, like, fly into your face.
I think *Breaking Dawn* should just be a normal movie, but who
knows. Watch, it's going to end up being a 3D movie —
'No, it's a great idea, it's a great idea!'"
— Kristen considers the *Breaking Dawn* in 3D question

and the Deathly Hallows was with its first part in November 2010 and the second in July 2011. Stephenie Meyer suggested that approach herself, saying "... it's hard to imagine it fitting into 90 minutes. The book is just so long! I can't imagine how to distill it — if I could, the book would be shorter. But maybe a screenwriter can see a way to do it and still cover the crucial plot points." Fans weighed in on the one film or two issue, as did some cast members, like Peter Facinelli who felt two films would better serve the subject matter. Trying to be diplomatic while doing interviews for *The Yellow Handkerchief*, Kristen said, "The story definitely warrants two films, but, you know ... I'm sort of not supposed to have a feeling about this!"

Producer Wyck Godfrey, from Summit Entertainment, said the decision would be made once they saw the *Breaking Dawn* treatment. "The issue [of whether there will be one or two movies] is not going to be resolved until we get the full treatment and see whether it's organic. If it's not organic, I don't think it will be done, and if it is, it will be. It really has to do with how much level of detail from the book there is, with all of these new vampires that appear in *Breaking Dawn*, the whole section about Jacob. . . . It's a very long single movie if it does become a single movie." After some rumors circulated that Stephenie Meyer was upset with the studio over the two-parter question, she clarified her position on her website, "Two or one, whichever way fits the story best is fine by me, and everyone I've spoken with at Summit seems to feel the same way. We're all excited to move forward on this, and we are slowly and surely getting there." If

Breaking Dawn were split into two movies, Summit would have the additional task of negotiating contracts with its star actors, who signed on to do four films, not five.

Godfrey addressed the Renesmee question in an interview with the *LA Times*: "I keep having visions of Benjamin Button in my head. It's certainly going to be visual effects in some capacity along with an actor. I wouldn't be surprised if it ends up being a full CG creation, but it also may be a human shot on a soundstage that then is used to shrink down. I don't know. We need a director. When we get a director, that director will need to come with a point of view of how they want to tackle it." Who would direct *Breaking Dawn* was another favorite question to puzzle over between the release of *New Moon* and *Eclipse*. After the first glimpses of *New Moon* were made public, Chris Weitz emerged as a frontrunner in the fans' minds to sit in the director's chair. Said Weitz at the time, "No official offer has been made [for *Breaking Dawn*]. The fans have been enthusiastic about the footage and the trailer, and the studio responds to that by feeling good about me. We'll have to see how people feel about the entire movie, not only the studio but the fans, before the verdict is out whether I direct number four. David Slade is doing a great job on the third film, and by the time that comes out, he'll be the flavor of the moment."

Finding the right director would be a big decision for Summit. Said Godfrey in January 2010, "We're just focused on the treatment and getting that right. At that point, we're going to see who's available and who's appropriate. It's such a complicated book because you have

the emotions and the intensity of the love story — so you need somebody who's just a wonderful director of actors — and yet it's really complicated from an action and visual effects standpoint. They've got to have both tools in their kit."

In late April, Summit finally announced Oscar-winner Bill Condon would direct the final two films; *Breaking Dawn would* be split in two, reportedly with Renesmee's birth ending the first part. Director and screenwriter Condon, the man responsible for *Gods and Monsters*, *Chicago*, and *Dreamgirls*, followed in the tradition of Hardwicke, Weitz, and Slade by writing a heartfelt letter to the Twilighters describing *Breaking Dawn* as "a final chapter in the best sense; not just wide in scope and scale, but emotionally charged and intense throughout." The release date for the first part was set for November 18, 2011, with production rumored to begin in November 2010. The team behind *Breaking Dawn* had a tight schedule but there was no time to waste. Vampires may not age, but the actors who portray them certainly do.

chapter 21

Team Twilight

Every successful media franchise has its devoted fans, but there are few with a fan base as polarized and vocal as Twilight. Breaking down the factions of Twilight's fandom can often seem as complicated as *Breaking Dawn*'s assembly of international vampires, with alliances in constant flux and new factions emerging daily.

The core of Twilight's fandom are the "Twilighters." They own every edition of the books, they have seen the movies dozens of times, and their houses are filled with Twilight merchandise. Some Twilighters are so extreme about their love of the series that their loyalty has earned them the moniker of "Twihards." Twihards are the über-fans, who eat, sleep, and breathe Twilight. Twihards are the fans who not only know Edward's and Bella's birthdays better than those of their own families, but also throw parties in their honor.

Since its inception, the term "Twihard" has spawned a Trekker vs. Trekkie type of divide, with some fans embracing the name as a badge of honor, while others see it as derisive and take offense at its use. But whatever name they choose to adopt for themselves, if the Twilighters are the corps of the army that is the Twilight fandom, the Twihards are its officers. They are the few, the proud, the sparkly, and the first to lead the charge when Twilight fans take up a cause.

Within the ranks of the Twilighters dwell another subset of fans: the Twilight Moms. When the series was first published, many of its older female fans became frustrated that they could only share their fandom with teenagers. Lisa Hansen was one such fan. Feeling isolated and wondering if perhaps she wasn't the only woman of her demographic who loved *Twilight* to the point of obsession, Lisa reached out to the internet and discovered that she was far from alone; the Twilight Moms community was born. TwilightMoms.com greets visitors with the message, "Fans of the Twilight series in OUR STAGE of life (whether you're a mom or not) now have a place where we can gather unashamed of our irrational obsession with vampires and werewolves." The community is over 36,000 members strong and has proven a force to be reckoned with in fandom.

As solidly as Twilighters have banded together against outsiders, there is one topic that never fails to turn fans against each other: the object of Bella Swan's affections. With few exceptions, the fandom is polarized between Team Edward and Team Jacob. To Team Edward, the canon pairing with the stoic, troubled, immortal 17-year-old is unquestionable. Team Jacob argues that Jacob's warmth, support, and wolfy exuberance should have won Bella away from her vampire swain. The two factions can be so vocal in their constant battle over Bella's heart that it's very easy to miss the much smaller Team Switzerland: those fans who don't care who Bella ends up with as long as a good romance is involved. The animosity between Team Edward and Team Jacob is so heated that the merchandisers picked up on it; one can find scores of officially licensed Team Edward or Team Jacob shirts, hats, keychains, backpacks, water bottles, and buttons decorating any store at which teenagers are target customers.

Lurking on the periphery of the Twilight fandom are the lolfans. Though their actual

Kellan Lutz, along with Bronson Pelletier, greets fans at *Much on Demand* in Toronto.

feelings toward the books range from dedicated love to impassioned enmity, a lolfan's primary reason for reading the Twilight series and watching the films is the amusement they derive from them. Their poster child is Cleolinda Jones, who is responsible for introducing the terms "lolfan," "fursplosion," and "sparklepire" into the common fandom vocabulary, and whose summaries of the books and "Movies in 15 Minutes" parodies have been mentioned by media bloggers ranging from *New York* magazine to *Time*. Not only is she the reigning Queen of Twilight Snark, Cleolinda is also the embodiment of the lolfan who loves the books despite, or perhaps even because of, their perceived flaws. She compares her love for Twilight to cake: "I'm not going to defend [the Twilight books] any more than I'm going to defend Twinkies — you go and get yourself a Twinkie when you have a very specific kind of craving. . . . If you want gourmet pastry, or even a homemade cake, you know where to get that. If you're eating a Twinkie, you clearly know what you want and why you're eating it, and you know that it's not good to eat very many of them, but . . . you know . . . sometimes you just *want* one."

Be they Twihards or lolfans, Twilight Moms or teenagers, there is one thing common to all these factions of the fandom: few things can arouse their passion, joy, or ire so well or so strongly as Twilight.

For more evidence of just how devoted the fans are, enter the world of fan fiction. Stephenie Meyer's four-and-a-half books (including the *Midnight Sun* manuscript) have inspired a staggering 130,000-plus fan fiction stories. Simply explained, fan fiction (or fanfic or ff) is a story written by a fan based on the characters and often using the situations of an original work. For Twilight fan fiction, the original material consists of the four-and-a-half novels, the film adaptations, and the handful of additional excerpts provided by Stephenie Meyer on her website. This is the Twilight canon. Twilight fan fiction runs the gamut from authors who write alternate versions of the original plots to authors writing completely new stories as far removed from the original canon as imaginable. Some of these stories don't even feature vampires or werewolves; Edward, Bella, Jacob, and the Cullens are recast as everything from rock stars to survivors of the attack on Pearl Harbor.

Universally acclaimed as the greatest Twilight fan fiction story of them all is "Wide Awake" by Angstgoddess003. As she's mentioned in various interviews, her disappointment with *Breaking Dawn* was so great that she felt compelled to write her own version of the story. It's available on her Livejournal site and a modified, less sexually explicit version is available on fanfiction.net. "Wide Awake" has spawned its own collection of rabid fans who feel, as blogger Aura Illumina described, that "Wide Awake" is "the most addictive, different, broadening, baffling, emotion raising, thought triggering, profound, penetrating, delicious, touching, rich in depth psychology, multidimensional, realistic, absorbing, compelling, rousing, and freaking HOT fan fiction story I have ever read. Did I say the best? Well, it is."

The Twilight fan fiction community has made such an impact that high-profile authors (including Psymom, Angstgoddess003, EZRocksAngel, Bethaboo, Ninapolitan, Manyafandom, americnxidiot, bella c'ella luna, and tby789) presented an official panel at Comic-Con to discuss their stories, process, and ideas. Even the Twilight films' cast is aware of the large volume of writing featuring their characters. Kellan Lutz admits that he hasn't read any of the Emmett-centric fan fic-

tion but is pleased to know that it exists. "There's so much depression [right now] it's kind of cool to be part of something people are using as an escape. In a way, that's what Stephenie did — she had a dream and just elaborated on it and it's really encouraging that people are doing the same, and making it this journey." Ashley Greene agrees, "That's why people love it so much — you can take it and make what you want from it. That's why people are going, 'It's 8 to 80.' Before, it was very much a teenage girl demographic and now it's women of any age, and guys are starting to join in too, and it's because there's that element of fantasy. Literally, if you're 8 years old you look at it one way and if you're 80 you look at it another. . . . People are making connections over this film and over this book. You know, there's mothers and daughters and grandmas who can all sit and talk about this story, and all fantasize about it, and I think it's a really cool thing — it's rare." When asked whether he was aware of the large volume of erotic fan fiction, some of it featuring his character, Kellan responded, "I would love to read that! That's right up my alley."

Beyond the fan fiction community, perhaps one of the most enthusiastic groups in Twilight culture are the crafters who express their love for the series by creating knitted, quilted, painted, and bejewelled testaments to their favorite vampires and werewolves. Vast communities of Twilight crafters thrive on Livejournal, Ravelry, Flickr, and Craftster. Within days of the release of the *Twilight* movie, crafters were creating their own versions of the knitwear, particularly Bella's mittens and Rosalie's scarf. Jewellers have

(1) (2) (3)

(4) (5)

STUPID LAMB

Twicrafts!
(1) Team Jacob journal (Nikki Pitcher,
pitchmom.etsy.com); (2) replica of Bella's mittens (Erin Nicole Smith); (3) replica of Bella's
moonstone ring (Desiree, fallenhearts.net);
(4) Twilight-themed pillow (Lisa Kramer-
Leggett, lisateatime.blogspot.com);
(5) "Stupid Lamb" cross stitch (Flor
Hernandez); (6) Edward-themed necklace
(Paula McDonough, venbead.etsy.com); (7,
opposite) Twilight Mystery Quilt in progress.

(6)

what if
i'm the
bad guy

(7)

jumped on the bandwagon too, forging their own versions of Bella's moonstone ring and turquoise bracelet. There are even artists carving tiny wooden wolves like the one on the bracelet Jacob gives to Bella in *Eclipse*.

Flor Hernandez adapted her Edward cross stitch from a free pattern offered online by *The Guardian*. She says, "I love the Twilight books and Robert Pattinson, but must admit I am annoyed by the slight stupidity of the Bella character. I mean, she's dating a stalker who admits that he spies on her and wants to kill her. So, 'Stupid Lamb' is a tribute, both to the infamous stupid lamb quote in the novel and my general feelings for the character. I gave

Edward red eyes to signify he'd given in to his passions and dispatched Bella. This was also an inside joke for my best friend and I, since we constantly poke fun at ourselves for being grown women who love Twilight." More of Flor's work is posted on her personal craft blog, unafloresita.blogspot.com, and her writing is on embroidery blog FeelingStitchy.com.

Heather Ladick of Zeppelin Threads Quilt Shop is the creator of another impressive Twilight project, the Twilight Mystery Quilt. After noticing that many of her customers loved Twilight, she decided to create a tribute project to pass the time between the release of the first two movies: "It actually drew over 110 worldwide participants! I had women (and men) from many countries participating and waiting for each new set of instructions. No one knew what the finished production would look like." Based on the story in *Twilight*, instruction for quilt blocks were released in stages, each one symbolically representing a part of the narrative. Instructions for the Twilight Mystery Quilt can be found for free at zeppelinthreads.com.

As much as Stephenie Meyer has given to Twilight fans, Twilight fans have given back to the community at large through their participation in numerous charitable organizations.

fAN fICTIONARY

Deciphering the codes of fan fiction.

AH (all human): You won't find any vampires, werewolves, or other supernatural beings here. Darn.

A/N: Author's note.

Angst: Refers to stories that center on the emotional suffering of one or more characters. Also referred to as H/C (hurt/comfort), this is a popular category in fan fiction where one or more characters will be hurt, emotionally or physically, and other characters will try to comfort the victim.

AU (alternate universe): Not all fan fiction is set in the vampire and werewolf world of Twilight. AU is a signal that the story is set in an alternate universe. For example, Bella is a famous actor and Edward is hired as her publicist.

Beta: An editor who proofreads and generally fixes up a story, giving the writer advice on plot and characterization, before it's posted online.

Canon: Anything that appeared in the novels or movies which can therefore be "proven" to be a genuine aspect of the Twiverse or a character.

Crossover: Two fan fictions for the price of one! For example, Edward is a student at Hogwarts. Swoon.

Fluff: The opposite of angst. This refers to stories that are lighthearted, sweet, sometimes funny, and usually feature requited love.

HEA: Happily ever after.

Lemons/limes: Refers to degrees of "mature" content in fan fiction. A lemon denotes a story contains explicit descriptions of sexual acts whereas a lime has somewhat less explicit sexual content.

OC (original character): An OC is one of the author's creation and not a character that was created by Stephenie Meyer.

OOC (out of character): OOC warns readers that characters won't be quite the same as they are in Meyer's world. For instance, Bella might a social butterfly instead of a clumsy and shy girl. Or Edward could be a super hot awesome professional pianist. Oh wait, that's not that out of character.

Slash: Slash fiction originated in *Star Trek* fan fiction that featured a romance between Kirk and Spock; it identifies a romantic pairing of a same-sex couple.

Peter Facinelli, Kristen Stewart, and a cozy Nikki Reed take the time to pose for photos with Vancouverite Allie Henzel (left) and friends.

The largest and most well known of these endeavors is TheFandomGivesBack.com. The organization — run by three women prominent in the fan community, Nina, Lo, and Christina — auctions fan-made art, fan fiction, and other Twilight-related items. All the money raised is donated to Alex's Lemonade Stand Foundation (alexslemonade.org), created in honor of Alex Scott, and in support of finding a cure for cancer.

"There are *thousands* of pages of fan fiction that people have written about these characters because they matter to them as much as they matter to me."

– Stephenie Meyer

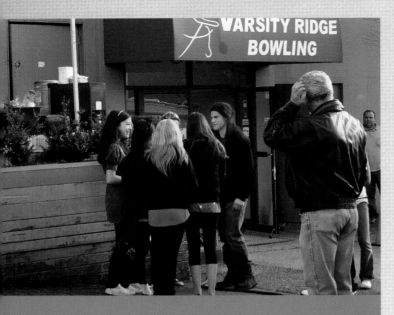

Taylor takes a break from filming to chat with fans gathered outside a *New Moon* location.

Fandom Gives Back has also teamed up with affiliate organizations such as Pattinson Online, Thinking of Rob, and @Pattinson411 in a worldwide effort to collect donations for victims of the Haiti earthquake. Rising to the call for fundraising initiatives, fan fiction author MsKathy issued a challenge to all fan fiction writers and readers: for every $5 donated to any charity in aid of Haiti, MsKathy would deliver a specially written story by email. Other high-profile fan fiction authors took up the idea and over 50 authors contributed stories. It was anticipated that this venture will raise as much as $10,000 for Haiti relief.

It's not just fans, but also Twilight cast members who have shown a fierce charitable spirit. Peter Facinelli launched a charitable endeavor, Twihards4Charity.com. Writes Peter on its website, "Twihards4Charity is about uniting the millions of Twilight fans and putting their power toward making a difference where it's needed the most. We are connecting brands, sponsors, and celebrities to provide Twilight-themed products that you love to benefit charity." Other cast members, from Kristen Stewart to Rachelle Lefevre, have used their fame for charitable purposes, raising money and awareness for good causes.

The fans are the reason the franchise has become such a huge phenomenon, and the people involved in creating the movies are well aware and appreciative of that. Rob Pattinson, for one, is not intimidated by individual Twilight fans but sometimes finds a group of screaming girls feels like an "ambush." When the first wave of his superstardom hit during the *Twilight* promotional tour, he wasn't prepared for his own reaction to it. Said Pattinson, he "would have thought your ego gets bigger with people screaming 'I love you' all the time but it's, like, the opposite effect. The more people scream . . . the more you just want to say, like, listen just don't. . . . You just feel like there's just so much more you have to live up to." Hearing crowds screaming is an "emotional experience" for Rob and his initial instinct was to start crying. He calls his response "really strange, [and] not how I thought I'd react." Kristen Stewart also acknowledges how surreal it is to be at the center of such an impassioned fandom. "This is exceptional," says the actress. "I'll never have this experience again no matter what kind of movie I make."

While the cast is happy to meet the fans and talk about their work, it is tiresome to be chased by paparazzi and have their personal lives the subject of such intense scrutiny. Said Kristen of the misleading sense that her every move is captured by cameras: "If every move *was* documented then there would be no false impression. . . . But it's all these isolated little moments — it looks so much crazier from an outsider's perspective. I don't live this, like, asinine, out of control, like manic crazy life. It's so focused on the work." A lot of the gossip media's coverage is on the "are they or aren't they" question of Rob and Kristen's relationship — are they just friends or is their on-screen chemistry a reflection of true love off-screen? Says *New Moon* director Chris Weitz, "People always want the stars of movies to fall in love with one another. There's no calculated effort to make it seem that way on the part of Summit marketing. You really want it to be about the characters themselves. It neither helps nor hurts [the films' success]. It just gives fans waiting in between movies something to talk about."

Not only curious about "Robsten," fans were also talking about the actors' other projects, and supporting the Twilight cast in all they do. When Kristen Stewart's *Welcome to the Rileys* looked like it was in danger of never seeing the light of day, Twilighters immediately jumped on the case, emailing distributors to say they would go see the movie in the theaters. Guest appearances from a Cullen or a wolf pack member is sure to get great ratings for a show or attention for an event. And Hollywood noticed the fandom's loyalty, and the actors benefited from being hot commodities. In the post–*New Moon* frenzy, for example, Taylor Lautner picked up leading roles in four films, including *Stretch Armstrong*, *Max Steel*, and *Cancun*, which is co-produced by Taylor's dad, Dan Lautner.

Twilighters were also treated to a graphic novel adaptation of their beloved *Twilight*. Released in March 2010 by Yen Press, *Twilight: The Graphic Novel, Volume 1* was illustrated by Young Kim and, like all offshoots of *Twilight*, was overseen by Stephenie Meyer. In a huge compliment to the artist, Stephenie told *EW*, "It's been a while since I was really able to read *Twilight*; there is so much baggage attached to that book for me now. It seems like all I can see are the mistakes in the writing. Reading Young's version brought me back to the feeling I had when I was writing and it was just me and the characters again. I love that. I thank her for it."

With dolls, posters, bedding, jewelry, life-sized cutouts, wardrobe replicas, board games, journals, and pretty much every piece of merchandise imaginable (both licensed and unofficial), fans still can't get enough of this extraordinary love story, creating their own stories and crafts to celebrate their fandom. And this insatiable desire is the greatest testament to the characters and story that Stephenie Meyer created from a powerful dream that has since made millions of people fall unconditionally and irrevocably in love with the Twilight Saga.

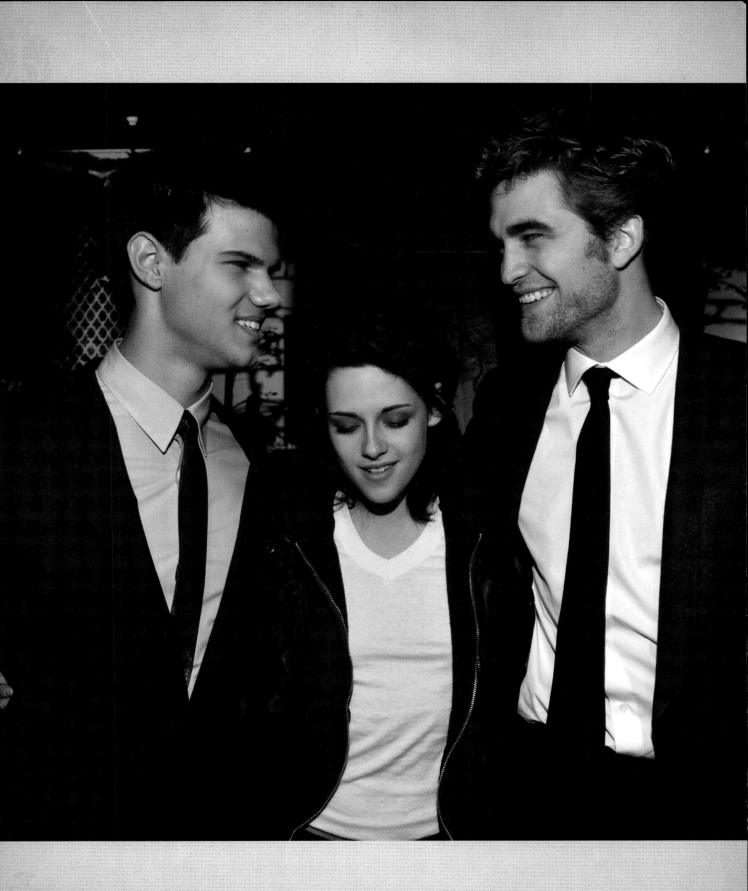

sink your teeth into these vamptastic books

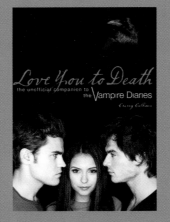

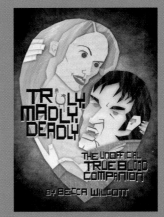

Bite Me!
The Unofficial Guide
to the World of Buffy
the Vampire Slayer

Love You to Death
The Unofficial Companion to
The Vampire Diaries

Truly, Madly, Deadly
The Unofficial
True Blood Companion

also available from ECW

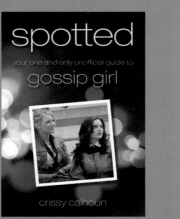

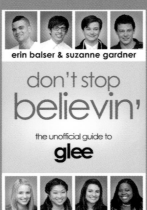

visit ecwcrew.wordpress.com for all the news on our upcoming books!